PACK UP YOUR TROUBLES

Pack
Up Your Troubles

A Collection of Verse

Edited by T E D   M A L O N E

Drawings by R OBERT S. R OBISON

GARDEN CITY PUBLISHING CO., INC.

GARDEN CITY, NEW YORK

Printed in the United States of America

Among the many distinguished persons who contributed stories and favorite poems to this book, I want especially to thank

Sen. Alva B. Adams
Amos 'n Andy
C. S. Anderson
Rev. Rufus Ansley
Faith Baldwin
Hon. Phil A. Bennett
Joan Blaine
Rev. Richard F. Blyer
Hon. Clarence J. Brown
Katherine Brush
Eddie Cantor
Sen. Arthur Capper
Gov. Chase A. Clark
Rev. Arthur M. Clarke
Hon. Cliff Clevenger
Marion Colman
Hon. Carl T. Curtis
Linda Darnell
Margaret Marshall Dean
Marlene Dietrich
Gordon Dorrance
Eddie Dowling
Mignon Eberhardt
Gov. Samuel C. Ford
Sen. Guy M. Gillette
Gov. Dwight Griswold
Rev. T. G. Hartwig
Roy C. Helfemden
Hon. Joseph Hendricks
Hon. Knute Hill
Hon. William S. Hill
Henry Hull
Rev. Stanley A. Hunter
June Hynd
Hon. Thomas A. Jenkins
Hon. Ben F. Jensen
Sen. E. L. Johnson

Brenda Joyce
H. V. Kaltenborn
Alma Kitchell
Lewis E. Lawes
Emil Lengyel
Ludwig Lewisohn
Elias Lieberman
Howard Lindsay
Luigi Lucioni
Dr. Ralph H. Lutz
Mary Margaret McBride
Gordon MacCreagh
Elizabeth MacGregor
Douglas MacLean
Dr. J. T. Madden
Rev. John Mantay
Fredric March
Elsa Maxwell
Ward Melville
George Montgomery
Victor Moore
Rev. Louie D. Newton
Sen. Gerald P. Nye
Hon. William T. Pheiffer
Gov. Leon C. Phillips
Sen. Louis Rabout
Sen. George L. Radcliffe
Margaret Reinhold
Gov. Leverett Saltonstall
Dorothy Stickney
Reba A. Swicegood
Lenore Ulric
Gov. Murray D. Van Wagoner
Hon. Albert Vreeland
William Allen White
Dorothy Wilson
Loretta Young

v

Contents

-->>|<<-

I. FIRST CALL

First Call

YOU'LL never know how near this book came to dying an untimely death just before it was begun. I made the almost fatal mistake of telling one of my pessimistic friends that I was planning a new book of poems for folks at home and fellows in camp. "Poems?" he exclaimed, his face breaking into the radiant smile of one who has just downed a glass of vinegar. "Poems? And pray tell me, Pollyanna, is poetry really good for anything besides fanning a steaming cup of four o'clock tea or lighting a hearth fire on a winter morning?"

Our laws protect such creatures from the deaths they deserve, so I took the crumbs he had tossed and spread them before the vulture as though he had been a canary. "What greater virtue, my fine feathered friend," I inquired, "than to temper them thar scalding moments and set a new flame glowing on last night's cold ashes?" My brilliant reply impressed him like a sour pickle. He urged me not to do it . . . it was a mistake. He was quite certain poetry was as out of date as petticoats. Finally, climaxing his plea, he flung at me:

> A wise old owl sat in an oak
> The more he saw the less he spoke
> The less he spoke the more he heard
> Why can't you be like that old bird?

From vultures to canaries to owls, all in one minute. I could have indulged in a little taxidermy and reminded the stuffed shirt that he had just quoted a verse to prove his point, and thus completely disproved it. But

there is another verse about the wisdom of knowing
a man is a cuckoo, and the foolhardiness of proving it
to him, so I reached for the crumbs again. I told my
alum-minded cynic that the verse about the owl was
one of Woodrow Wilson's favorites. He appeared surprised. Observing that he was impressed, I added that
it was also Calvin Coolidge's code of living. This wasn't
true, but it was so appropriate I couldn't resist it.
Following up my advantage I recklessly associated a
dozen more verses with important people until the
skeptic seemed almost ready to acknowledge that a
petticoat might still exist outside museums.

Then I had an idea. Why not a book filled with poems
of unusual significance, poems that have influenced
people in making important decisions, poems with
strength to cool the desperate passions that burn all
the hope and faith out of our beings, and poems that glow
like magic lanterns in the dusk? The world is full of
poetry . . . orators quote it to stir an audience to
action . . . black men on the levee chant it as their
muscles swell in unison . . . cheering sections throb
with it, beating victory out of defeat . . . mothers sing
it in the lullabies at bedtime. Its words are woven from
the dreams of men, its rhythm from their hearts. This
is the stuff of life, of all our lives. These are the poems
that serve as songs, serve men on the march. Somewhere
up ahead a strong voice starts singing . . . others join
in and soon, like a fire sweeping up the mountainside,
the whole column is striding forward to the ringing
words, "Pack up your troubles . . . ."

It was a good idea and because I believed it would
make a good book I went to work to build one. I began
hunting back through my files for letters and stories
from people telling how certain poems had helped them
make important decisions, letters describing how other
poems had been a quiet influence throughout their days

of trouble. Then I wrote to hundreds of people all over America asking if poetry had contributed to their success. The response was more than gratifying . . . it was overwhelming. The vast majority I have had to leave out, some because the stories were so unusual I was actually afraid people would not believe them, others because of the obvious limitations of space, but those included, I hope, will represent all the readers of poetry, the casual, the earnest, and the scholarly. No claim is made that every poem is a miracle, but simply that in one way or another all have contributed to the sum total of happiness in the world. So read the book. Read it like a story or an anthology or, better yet, let each page be the beginning of a song. Then you can join in the melody flowing through your heart and the words will help you—"Pack Up Your Troubles."

2. REVEILLE

Reveille

->»«<-

I DON'T know how it happened, but somewhere across the way I heard the clear high notes of a bugle, then the hurdy-gurdy man down the street began grinding out "Pack Up Your Troubles," and suddenly it seemed so exactly the right thing to do, I stalked into a tobacco shop, bought me a big pipe, and shuffled out, a philosopher.

Discovering a little boy down on his knees howling to high heaven as he peered through the iron grating in the walk, I cheerily sang out, "Don't worry, son, every cloud has a silver lining." But he was unimpressed; in fact he bawled even louder as he turned on me. "I don't want no silver up there; I just want my nickel down here!" That mistake cost me five cents. And I had just about decided to knock the ashes out of my pipe and admit defeat when a young chap wandered up and sat down on the curbing. It was so perfectly timed it seemed providential; here, surely, was a fellow philosopher. I could sit down beside him, hang my feet over the edge of the world, and together we could solve all the problems of society. "Sorry, Buddy, I'm looking for a job. A guy's gotta be a magician to succeed these days! Can you spare the price of a cup of coffee?" I successfully conjured up the amount necessary to start him off for "java." But intrigued, if not enchanted, by his casual remark, I remained there seated on the curbstone thinking: "A magician!" "Magic!" That didn't sound so bad; so I relit my pipe and became a magician.

There are all kinds of magic formulas and some can be explained and some can't. Nearly everyone has seen a genial magician wave his wand over an empty high silk hat, mutter some mysterious little verse, and lift a big fat rabbit out of the yawning nothingness within. I am assured by my skeptical friends that that can be explained. One in the "know" even went so far as to whisper the mysterious words to me—"Sim-Sali-Bim." But there must have been some mistake. I borrowed a hat and tried it—not even a moth jumped out. There are other verses, other formulas. There is a small black box in a little town in Idaho into which one can say a few words and almost immediately people a thousand, two thousand, or even ten thousand miles away can be heard talking. I understand the "Sim-Sali-Bim" of that trick is a different chant. For that magic you say, "Long Distance, get me New York City, please," and after a breathless pause and the contribution of sufficient nickels and dimes and quarters in the proper places, you can hear a voice as plain as day saying, "This is New York." Again I'm told that that one can be explained, but after the telephones are all taken apart and the wires untangled, my informer comes to the word electricity and that word seems to be just as mysterious as the old word "magic." Radio does the trick without wires. A magician I know can produce a rabbit without a hat. Science or sleight of hand, it's a good trick if you can do it.

I know a little fellow who pushed his button nose flat against a rain-wet window one autumn afternoon and recited the only magic he knew:

> Rain, rain, go away.
> Come again some other day.
> Little Johnny wants to play.

And he did too, and it did too, and he went out and played. I'll admit some weather men aren't such good magicians, but weather is a good trick when it works, and so are apple pies and long-distance calls and, for that matter, rabbits.

There are all kinds of magic formulas and some can be explained and some can't. Nobody knows why the thin weird wail of reed will charm a hated cobra into a spell, leaving him as helpless as a weaving coil of rope. Nobody can explain why the swift beat of drums in a big brass band will arouse a tired army and set it marching again. Nostalgic old songs will set a crowd of strangers singing together arm in arm. Music, like poetry, is a magic formula and it can do as many tricks as "Abracadabra," "Hocus Pocus," or "Sim-Sali-Bim." All you have to know is the right chant to use to work the spell and "Mumbo-Jumbo," "Open Sesame," "Wish I may, wish I might, First star I've seen tonight"—and whether you understand it or not, it works. It sounds like a game, and in a way it is. It is the exciting game we all call living. And when you realize how much magic there is in everything that happens, how many impossible things become possible when you have the courage to believe . . . well . . . .

->>)((<-

If you want a thing bad enough
To go out and fight for it,
Work day and night for it,
Give up your time and your peace and your sleep for it
If only desire of it
Makes you quite mad enough
Never to tire of it,
Makes you hold all other things tawdry and cheap for it
If life seems all empty and useless without it
And all that you scheme and you dream is about it,
If gladly you'll sweat for it,
Fret for it,

Plan for it,
Lose all your terror of God or man for it,
If you'll simply go after that thing that you want,
With all your capacity,
Strength and sagacity,
Faith, hope and confidence, stern pertinacity,
If neither cold poverty, famished and gaunt,
Nor sickness nor pain
Of body or brain
Can turn you away from the thing that you want,
If dogged and grim you beseige and beset it,
You'll get it!

—Berton Braley.

->»«<-

For ten years I have been playing with the magic of poetry, its curious charms and enchantments. People in all walks of life, in thousands of towns and cities, have sent in nearly a million verses and poems with elaborate stories and positive assurances of their unfailing power. Some of them have worked, some of them have not, but a few have worked like magic.

->»«<-

A book could be written about Kipling's "If." Every schoolboy has read it, any taxi driver can quote it. Governors of nearly every state have at one time or another proclaimed it their favorite. Recently Governor Murray D. Van Wagoner of Michigan remarked, "I had occasion to recall this poem for one solid week when I was settling the Ford strike as chief mediator between the Ford Company and the CIO—especially that part of the poem . . . 'If you can keep your head when all about you are losing theirs and blaming it on you . . . .'" Newspaper editors, ministers, businessmen —all have spoken of the influence of "If" in their lives.

On the stage Lenore Ulrich and Henry Hull are two of the many actresses and actors who have been spurred through discouragement by the promise of justice in this singing challenge. But if these testimonies are not enough, here is a dramatic story from Marlene Dietrich's own pen:

"It was the winter of 1918 in Berlin," Miss Dietrich wrote, "and my coming upon 'If' then gave me a philosophy and comfort which helped during the most trying days of my life."

She recalled it was the time of Germany's realization and shock that it had lost the World War; food was acutely scarce; the country had been starved insensible, except to the rigors of one of the worst winters northern Europe had experienced in years.

Further, only a few weeks before, the girl had learned of her father's death in fierce action on the Russian front. She had no brothers or sisters. She and her mother, quite penniless, were trying to find a new footing in revolution-crazed, famine-ridden Berlin.

"One morning, on my way to the food depot where we stood in line for milk and bread, I had to pass a baker's shop. Rioters had broken in the night before. Glass was all over the roped-off sidewalk. Such sights were common in Berlin, but as I stopped to look I saw a little framed picture in the rubbish which had spilled outside. It was a poem, and I could clearly read only the first line: 'If you can keep your head when all about you are losing theirs and blaming it on you. . . . '

"A year or so later I managed to get a copy of the complete poem. I have always treasured it. I must have six or seven embossed copies of the work at home, presented by friends who knew I liked it. 'If' helped me through the most critical period of my life. Once a great source of encouragement, it is still that and, in addition, a nostalgic pleasure."

IF

If you can keep your head when all about you
   Are losing theirs and blaming it on you,
If you can trust yourself when all men doubt you,
   But make allowance for their doubting too;
If you can wait and not be tired by waiting,
   Or being lied about, don't deal in lies,
Or being hated don't give way to hating,
   And yet don't look too good, nor talk too wise:

If you can dream—and not make dreams your master;
   If you can think—and not make thoughts your aim;
If you can meet with Triumph and Disaster
   And treat those two impostors just the same;
If you can bear to hear the truth you've spoken
   Twisted by knaves to make a trap for fools,
Or watch the things you gave your life to, broken,
   And stoop and build 'em up with worn-out tools:

If you can make one heap of all your winnings
   And risk it on one turn of pitch-and-toss,
And lose, and start again at your beginnings
   And never breathe a word about your loss;
If you can force your heart and nerve and sinew
   To serve your turn long after they are gone,
And so hold on when there is nothing in you
   Except the Will which says to them: "Hold on!"

If you can talk with crowds and keep your virtue,
   Or walk with Kings—nor lose the common touch,
If neither foes nor loving friends can hurt you,
   If all men count with you, but none too much;
If you can fill the unforgiving minute
   With sixty seconds' worth of distance run,

Yours is the Earth and everything that's in it,
And—which is more—you'll be a Man, my son!
                              —Rudyard Kipling.

Yes, a dozen books could be filled with the stories of
"If" and its almost magic effect upon lives. I don't
know about its ability to pull a rabbit out of a high hat,
but I have vast evidence that it can produce a man out
of a "stuffed shirt."

→>≻≪←

Margaret Reinhold is one of America's outstanding
contenders for the national championship in fancy
diving. You might be surprised to know that poetry is
her springboard.

"In my five years of competition, I have won many
sectional diving titles throughout the United States.
. . . Before each and every meet I read this poem to
myself over and over again and in spite of my not yet
winning that much wanted first place in national
competition, I feel that my believing in this poem and
carrying it out to the best of my ability gives me much
greater victory.

Dear Lord, in the battle that goes on through life
A courage to strive and to dare;
And if I should win let it be by the code,
    With my faith and my honor held high,
And if I should lose let me stand by the road
    And cheer as the winners go by!"

→>≻≪←

Not all poems are charms or enchantments, of course;
there is all the ominous sorcery of caldrons and witches
in these four lines:

> Beware lest thou
> get what thou desire
> . . . and with it
> Hell Fire!

That's a good trick if you can avoid it.

-»»«<-

H. V. Kaltenborn owes his first job in New York City to this magic stuff called poetry. The first contribution he ever made to a newspaper at the age of nine ended with four rhymed lines. He protested to the editor of the *Merrill* (Wisconsin) *News* because his father was obliged to pay a monthly water rate despite the fact that most of the water lines were frozen up for the winter months by the biting frosts of northern Wisconsin. Thus this conclusion:

> If the water-works don't stop this,
>   On my house I'll paint "To Let,"
> And stop paying for the water
>   Which all winter I don't get.

But the most important poem Kaltenborn ever wrote was produced in the fall of 1902, when he was walking the streets of New York City in search of a newspaper job. Inspired by the sight of the vast crowds that poured toward the Manhattan end of the Brooklyn Bridge each evening, he wrote a paraphrase on Southey's "The Cataract of Lodore." The original poem describes the way the water pours over the cataract, and Kaltenborn described the gathering of the crowds at Manhattan and the manner in which they poured across the bridge. He can only recall the opening lines, which were:

> From the buildings that rise
> Till they reach to the skies

From twentieth floors
And department stores,
They walk, run and stop
Before a bright window
Then, suddenly starting
Again are departing
With hurrying feet
They race through the street.

That poem brought Kaltenborn the first and most precious compliment he has ever received from a newspaper editor. Gilbert Evans, then managing editor of the *Brooklyn Daily Eagle*, told him, "We don't usually pay for poetry, but if you'll go down to the cashier's window, you'll find $5.00 waiting for you. And if you want to start in working on stock tables, I'll give you a job at $8.00 a week."

That was the NBC commentator's poetical beginning in metropolitan journalism.

->>><<<-

I asked Dr. Ralph H. Lutz, professor of history at Stanford University, what poem had seemed most important in his life, and his answer, which did not carry the full approval of some of his poet friends, was Tennyson's "Ulysses." It was first read to him by his father, when he was a grammar-school student. "I recall that he read it to me in his study at Port Angelus, on the shores of the Straits of Juan de Fuca. From a distance, I could hear the firing of the guns from the British base at Esquimault.

I am a part of all that I have met;
Yet all experience is an arch where-thro'
Gleams that untravell'd world, whose margin fades
For ever and for ever when I move . . .

Tho' much is taken, much abides; and tho'
We are not now that strength which in old days
Moved earth and heaven; that which we are, we are.

"'I am a part of all that I have met' appealed to me
in childhood, youth, and now in middle life.

"These lines have many times added strength to my
own life. In 1904, I heard George Cram Cook, a late
American genius not yet fully discovered by his country-
men, read these lines to a crowded classroom of young
Stanford students. Ten years later, I heard Frank
Mason recite part of them in a bomb shelter in France,
while the German planes droned overhead."

-»>»<«-

An experience, really more miraculous than magic,
of Emil Lengyel, author and educator, belongs right here
exactly as he tells it in his letter:

"The time was: June 6, 1916.

"The place was: Somewhere in Russia, near the town
of Luck. (It's a real name.)

"The incident was: A hand grenade thrown into our
shelter by an enemy soldier with the intent to kill. A
couple of feet away it exploded and killed the man
standing next to me. The next hand grenade was there
already, meant for me. Then:

"The verse: 'Où sont les neiges d'antan.' I repeated
the words automatically: 'Where are the snows of
yester-year?' and I felt perfectly calm and unruffled.
François Villon probably never suspected what his line
would mean to a young soldier in distant times to
come."

Because this remarkable experience seems all the more
remarkable when the whole poem is read and the
significance of that haunting line "Where are the snows
of yester-year?" is more fully explained, here is the
Rossetti translation, which seems most appropriate:

THE BALLAD OF DEAD LADIES

Tell me now in what hidden way is
    Lady Flora the lovely Roman?
Where's Hipparchia, and where is Thais,
    Neither of them the fairer woman?
    Where is Echo, beheld of no man,
Only heard on river and mere—
    She whose beauty was more than human? . . .
But where are the snows of yester-year?

    .   .   .

White Queen Blanche, like a queen of lilies,
    With a voice like any mermaiden—
Bertha Broadfoot, Beatrice, Alice,
    And Ermengarde the lady of Maine—
    And that good Joan whom Englishmen
At Rouen doomed and burned her there—
    Mother of God, where are they then? . . .
But where are the snows of yester-year?

Nay, never ask this week, fair lord
    Where they are gone, nor yet this year,
Except with this for an overword—
    But where are the snows of yester-year?
                —Dante Gabriel Rossetti.

→→→»«←←←

A story that does not belong in this book but must
not be left out comes from Eddie Cantor, the magician
of laughter.

"I wasn't too good a student, back in my grammar
school days at P. S. #2. It was all (Heaven help me!)
terribly boring to a would-be actor. But I knew that I
had to make good, when each semester ended, and
students were to be promoted.

"There was a poem, hidden away in a nondescript little leather-covered book which I found in the Recreation Center Library. It seemed to me the very soul of tragedy, a piece that the 'ham' in me couldn't resist attempting. I learned the poem by heart, accompanied it with every Thespian gesture I could conceive, and recited it to our Principal, who, believe it or not, told me with tears in his eyes, that I must recite it at the graduation exercises.

"It was my biggest success. Women noisily wept, and men blew their noses loudly, as I whispered the last sad line, and, head bowed, walked off the stage. I was promoted to the next class.

"That poem saw me through three more graduation exercises. If I hadn't finally left school—by request, on another matter—I believe I myself would have graduated on the strength of my performance of

THE SOUL OF THE VIOLIN

It has come at last, old comrade,
It has come at last:
The time when you and I must say goodbye . . .

"Wouldn't you think that I could never forget that poem, after all the performances of it I gave? But lately, radio gags have taken the place of a lot of fond memories in my mind, and I'm afraid the rest of the poem is gone forever.

"Unless you, Ted Malone, manage to seek it out. I'd love to see it again. I'm sure that if you gave me the next line, I could sail through it with ease.

Cordially,
Eddie Cantor."

So, anxious to provide "the next line," I described over a coast-to-coast radio network Mr. Cantor's predicament, whereupon we were promptly deluged, flooded,

swamped with "Ghosts of the Violin." But shades of a
Stradivarius! The sheafs of papers, in longhand, short-
hand, typewritten, and in books themselves, bore no
poems at all. The "Soul of the Violin" was not a poem,
but a prose reading. (That's why the story has no right
to be in this book.) When I faced Mr. Cantor with this
surprising upset, his big eyes grew bigger and he calmly
replied, "My friend, when prose does what that piece
did for me, it is poetry."

->>>«<<-

There are all kinds of magic formulas—but a magician's best tricks are those he doesn't explain. So here
are pages and pages of poetry with only a hint of the
story hidden between the lines—poems that have actually
played more or less important parts in the lives of the
most interesting people. Don't let the brevity or sim-
plicity of a poem fool you. Some of the hardest tricks
look simplest, and most of them are when you have the
right formula. I can't promise every poem will work
like magic for you, but I can promise that if you will
make them a part of your life in this great glad adventure
of living you will soon discover how easy it is to "pack
up your troubles" and—pull out a rabbit.

3. ASSEMBLY

Assembly

❧❧❧❧

TWO BUILD A WORLD

Two build a world from dreams
   Each heart has known—
A cup and saucer, and a painted chair,
   Some ruffled curtains and a garden grown
Before the watchful eyes of two who care.
   From picnic suppers on a pasture hill
And books at dusk, and fudge and popcorn balls,
   From potted flowers on a window sill
And autumn moons and firelight on a wall.

Two build a world from lullabies at dark,
   And blocks and trains and cookies in a jar;
And secrets shared, and rambles in a park;
   From bedtime talks, and wishes on a star,
And daffodils and rosebuds tightly curled.
Of timber such as these, two build a world.
               —Frances Davis Adams.

TO A HUSBAND AND WIFE

Preserve sacredly the privacies of your own
house, your married state and your heart. Let
no father or mother or sister or brother ever
presume to come between you or share the joys
or sorrows that belong to you two alone.

With mutual help build your quiet world,
allowing your dearest earthly friends to be
the confidant of naught that concerns your
domestic peace. Let moments of alienation,
if they occur, be healed at once. Never, no
never, speak of it outside; but to each other
confess and all will come out right. Never
let the morrow's sun still find you at variance.
Renew and renew your vow. It will do you good;
and thereby your minds will grow together contented in that love which is stronger than death,
and you will be truly one.

—Unknown.

EARFUL FOR BRIDES

Just because your hair is curly,
And your teeth are white and pearly,
    And your figure's very lovely, and you're cute—
Don't imagine, for a minute,
That it's bunk, there's nothing in it,
    When I issue this grave warning—*feed the brute!*

Wedded bliss is very simple,
Just forget about your dimple,
    Mobilize your thoughts 'round hubby's inner man—
Study goulash and bolony,
And pigs' feet and macaroni,
    And get chummy with a pot and frying pan.

If you'd win a loyal booster,
Every Sunday boil a rooster,
    With a peck of noodles draped around its frame—
Feed him waffles smeared with honey,
And you've got his love and money,
    And you'll never need to fear some other dame.

Men are lugs and heels and sinners,
When they're hungry for their dinners,
    And just spoiling for a chance to bawl you out—
But they're mild beyond comparing
When they're gorged on pickled herring,
    Or their tummy's full of beans and sauerkraut.

Feed him, stuff him with potatoes,
Dumplings, ham hocks and tomatoes,
    And dish up a pan of cornbread, piping hot—
Give him pie and cake and custard,
And hot dogs well smeared with mustard,
    And don't ever fail to serve meals on the dot.

Never mind your swell complexion,
And your eyebrow's arched perfection,
    It's a kitchen apron now that makes you cute—
It's a sad fact, but don't doubt it,
For there's no two ways about it,
    If you'd have a happy marriage—*feed the brute!*
                                    —Unknown.

ONCE I WAS A BACHELOR

Oh, once I was a bachelor
    Untrammeled as the air;
I lived on fried potatoes
    And I seldom cut my hair,
My home was where I parked my pipe;
    My bank was in my pocket;
I always had a dollar watch
    Because I couldn't hock it.
A wild and wooly bachelor,
    I wandered wide and free,
And then a tiny Creature came
    Along and married me!

So long I'd been a bachelor
  It had become a habit,
So when a dollar came along
  And I reached out to grab it,
But found a smaller hand than mine,
  And defter, beat me to it . . .
Oh, when I was a bachelor
  All blithesomely I blew it!
But now the tiny Creature
  Shuts it in a prison dank,
A dark and dismal dungeon that
  They call a Savings Bank.

Oh, once I was a bachelor
  And didn't give a darn;
I NEVER meekly held my hands
  While Someone wound the yarn;
I turned my collars if I liked
  I bathed in summer weather,
And wore the same old outing shirt
  For days and days together . . .
A wild and wooly bachelor, as happy as could be;
Now listen to the awful things that happen unto me:

Every day a shoe shine;
  Twice a day a scrub;
Every night a toothbrush;
  Every morn a tub;
Twice a day a shampoo . . .
  Glub! Glub! Glub!
Once I was a bachelor . . .
  Now I am a Hub.
Hubby wants to loaf a bit;
  Hubby wants to shirk;
Hubby wants to ramble some . . .
  But Hubby's got to work!

Every morn a hot sprint
  For the eight o'clock;
Every week the pay check
  Goes into the sock.
Oh, once I was a bachelor and wandered wide and free;
Now I'm not a bachelor . . . and take a look at me!

And yet I've got a check book,
  A flivver and a home;
And there's a tiny Creature
  Who, when I start to roam
Is right there, close beside me,
  Every moment of the trip;
No longer does the porter
  Make a fortune from my tip.

She helps me fight my battles;
  She listens when I brag;
She keeps the ball a-rolling when
  Ambition wants to lag;
She comforts and consoles me,
  And, to save my very life,
I can't see how I once got on
  For years without a wife!
Oh, once I was a bachelor,
  And rolled 'em wide and high;
But now I'm NOT a bachelor . . .
  And I'm a lucky guy!

               —Lowell Otus Reese.

FREEDOM

  Like autumn leaves
    My buttons fall away
  My shirts and socks
    All haste to swift decay.

Bacon and toast
  Each morn I carbonize
They burst in flame
  If once I turn my eyes.

The faucets drip—
  They drip and never cease.
Each plate and dish
  Is filmed with horrid grease.

The bread-knife's cut
  My finger to the bone—
My wife's away,
  I'm keeping house alone.
                    —John F. Haylock.

THE SUBMERGED HUSBAND

Husband and wife, husband and wife!
By love and the law united for life.
By love and the law through the years we have gone
Until we are really and truly just one.
Oh, list to the glorious tale of our life,
I'm a husband who's truly submerged in his wife.
Yes, truly submerged in the love we have known,
And, no longer, I think, I've a mind of my own.

"Will you have some more pie?" says my hostess to me,
"No thank you, he doesn't wish more," answers she,
"A bit of cheese?" "Shall I pass you the knife?"
"Don't bother, he never eats cheese," says the wife.
"Will you have some more coffee?" ere I can look up
"No thank you," she says, and I put down my cup.
I don't have to express my opinion, you see
For the wife is right there with an answer for me.

It's a trifle embarrassing oft I confess
If the wife answers "no" when I'd like to say "yes."
But time has reduced my resentment somehow
She has done it so long that I'm used to it now.
No longer I mind it, no longer I think
Of matters pertaining to food or to drink,
We are one, we are one, as our friends all agree
And the missus does all of the talking for me.
                                        —Unknown.

IF WE DIDN'T HAVE TO EAT

Life would be an easy matter
    If we didn't have to eat.
        If we never had to utter,
        "Won't you pass the bread and butter,
Likewise push along that platter
    Full of meat?"
        Yes, if food were obsolete
        Life would be a jolly treat,
If we didn't—shine or shower,
Old or young, 'bout every hour—
        Have to eat, eat, eat, eat, eat—
        'Twould be jolly if we didn't have to eat.

We could save a lot of money
    If we didn't have to eat.
        Could we cease our busy buying,
        Baking, broiling, brewing, frying,
Life would then be oh, so sunny
    And complete;
        And we wouldn't fear to greet
        Every grocer in the street
If we didn't—man and woman,
Every hungry, helpless human—
        Have to eat, eat, eat, eat, eat—
        We'd save money if we didn't have to eat.

All our worry would be over
　　If we didn't have to eat.
　　　　Would the butcher, baker, grocer
　　　　Get our hard-earned dollars? No, Sir!
We would then be right in clover
　　Cool and sweet.
　　　　Want and hunger we could cheat,
　　　　And we'd get there with both feet,
If we didn't—poor or wealthy,
Halt or nimble, sick or healthy—
　　　　Have to eat, eat, eat, eat, eat,
　　　　We could get there if we didn't have to eat.
　　　　　　　　　　　　　　—Nixon Waterman.

BILL OF FARE

Men eat at different places,
　　According to their salaries,
And feed their various faces
　　With vitamins and calories.
Some raise a cry for ham and eggs, while some eat
　　shredded hay,
But the basis of their diet is the Speaker of the Day.

Though viands sweetly savor,
　　Though silverware be glistening,
Our business men must favor
　　The simple art of listening.
They hurry through the eating part as quickly as they
　　may,
And raise expectant faces to the Speaker of the Day.

Exalted are their wishes,
　　They hunger mostly mentally,
They trifle with their dishes,
　　But only incidentally.

The noon hour finds them flocking to the handiest cafe—
But it's not the chef who lures them; it's the Speaker of
the Day.

We thus observe that eating
　Is highly educational,
For art is long, time fleeting,
　Addresses inspirational;
And it's the queer, eccentric chap who hides himself
　away,
And masticates his sirloin with no Speaker of the Day.
　　　　　　　　　　　　—Stoddard King.

METHUSELAH

Methuselah ate what he found on his plate,
　And never, as people do now,
Did he note the amount of the calory count;
　He ate it because it was chow.
He wasn't disturbed as at dinner he sat,
　Devouring a roast or a pie,
To think it was lacking in granular fat
　Or a couple of vitamins shy.
He cheerfully chewed each species of food,
　Unmindful of troubles or fears
Lest his health might be hurt
By some fancy dessert;
　And he lived over nine hundred years.
　　　　　　　　　　　　—Unknown.

→»×«←

I wish we had a little house
　With ivy vines along the wall,
A bright brass knocker on the door
　And leaded fanlight in the hall.
I wish it had a wide old hearth
　Where maple knots would roar and blaze

And we could sit and drink our tea
And read old books on Autumn days.
                    —Unknown.

PEACE

I could not ask a better world
    More innocent of follies
Than cool green lawns and friendly homes
    And men with pipes and collies
And little girls who sit on steps
    A-talking to their dollies.
                    —George Greenway.

THE HEART'S CORNER

A shaded candle set in a square of books,
    A bowl of roses—joy enough for one—
    A task completed and a task begun—
That's how my corner looks.

A mound of cushions heaped against the wall,
    A blowing curtain white and thin and sweet—
    My film of magic drawn against the street—
A chair, a desk or table—that is all.

Yet what a kingdom hath the heart in this,
    And what a fortress built against despair—
    Here may I bear the wrong too great to bear,
Here may I live again my hour of bliss.

Here are the puny woes and petty stings
    Of daily living banished and forgot,
    Through ancient palaces that now are not
I sit with princes and I talk with kings.

Here may I greet the world's great noblemen,
Whose words renew the hopes that late were chill.
The olden fire leaps up to light the will
And I am strong to meet the world again.
                            —Angela Morgan.

THE PUNISHING

I spanked a little boy last night
I thought that I was doing right,
I thought that I was punishing
A little boy for some wrong thing.
Today I bought a ball and kite
For that same boy I spanked last night,
Bought marbles, tops and everything
To counteract the punishing.
You see—through tears this little lad
Tried hard to smile and then said, "Dad,
Will spanking make me good like you?"
I think you would have bought things too.
                            —Unknown.

JUNIOR WRITES TO SANTA CLAUS

Dear Santa Claus, do you suppose
    That you could send to me,
Two trains with tracks this Christmas Eve
    If I'm as good as can be?

You see, Dear Mr. Santa Claus,
    My daddy likes to play
With all my things, but most of all
    He likes the tracks to lay!

Dear Santa Claus, if you can send
    Two trains, why don't you see,
My dad can play with his own train,
    And leave my train for me!
                            —Agnes Carr.

HE'S JUST A DOG

He's just a dog with a stumpy tail,
   And a moth-eaten coat of tan.
His legs are short, of the wobbly sort—
   I doubt if he ever ran.

He howls at night, yet in broad daylight
   He sleeps like a blooming log.
He likes the feed of the gutter breed
   Oh, he's an irregular dog.

I call him "Bum," and in total sum
   He is all that name implies,
For he's just a tramp of the highway stamp
   Which culture can not disguise.

His friends I found in the street abound
   Urchins, dogs and men.
Yet he sticks to me with fiendish glee
   Which is really beyond my ken.

I talk to him sometimes when I'm lonesome
   And I know that he understands,
For he listens to me attentively
   And then gently licks my hands.

He rubs his nose on my tailored clothes
   And I say naught thereat,
For the good Lord knows I can buy more clothes
   But never a friend like that.

So my dear old Pal,
   My moth-eaten, flea-bitten, stumpy-tail friend
You've made a part in my very heart
   To be cherished until the journey's end.

And if on Judgment Day I wend my way
  Toward the place where the righteous meet,
If my dog is barred by the Heavenly Guard
  Then we'll both of us brave the heat.
                                    —Unknown.

HALF-PAST TEARS

Over the pond and down the road,
  Pint and half-pint size,
Go the little girl with the broken doll
  And the dog with the sad, sad, eyes.

She had been spending the day with a friend,
  'Till dolly and she had a fall;
But the dog can't tell, so nobody knows
  Wherever he's been, at all!

Trudging along through the dust and the heat,
  Tragedy stalks their trail,
The doll has a broken head and the dog
  Has lost all the wag to his tail.

Maybe somebody can mend the doll,
  And lemonade's good for tears,
But what's to become of the sad, sad dog,
  With the cockle-burrs in his ears?
                                    —Edith Ogden.

MY DOG'S TAIL

What put the wiggle in a little dog's tail
  I'd like to know!
That gay little wiggle, that glad little waggle—
  How did it grow?

It starts in his mind and runs out behind
    To the tip of his tail, and then
That glad little waggle, that gay little wiggle
    Begins all over again.

The day may be sunny or dark with rain,
    The wiggle is there just the same;
It needs just a whistle to set it a-wiggle
    Or the sound of his favorite name.

No doubt I shall never, in any way ever
    Find out how that wiggle got there,
But I'm very sure, while tails shall endure,
    That tail will wig-wag in the air!
                        —Arthur Wallace Peach.

TWO IN ONE

When Pop's down at the office
    He's a mighty 'portant guy.
He growls his orders, loud and fierce,
    An' makes his 'ployees fly.
He's yessed by all, just like they think
    Whate'er Pop does is right.
When Pop's down at the office
    He's a man of main and might.

But when Pop's home, he's diffrunt;
    He hasn't much to say,
An' does just what my Mom tells 'im,
    An' does it my Mom's way.
Mom contradicts him quite a bit,
    An' keeps Pop on the hop.
Pop's a "big shot" at the office,
    But at home he's just a "pop."
                        —C. M. Andrews.

WHEN PA IS SICK

When Pa is sick, he's scared to death,
An' Ma an' us just holds our breath,
He crawls in bed, an' puffs an' grunts,
An' does all kinds of crazy stunts.
He wants "Doc" Brown and mighty quick,
For when Pa's ill he's awful sick.
He gasps an' moans, an' sort o' sighs,
He talks so queer, an' rolls his eyes,
Ma jumps an' runs, an' all us,
An' all the house is in a fuss,
An' peace and joy is mighty skeerce . . .
When Pa is sick it's something fierce.

WHEN MA IS SICK

When Ma is sick she pegs away,
She's quiet, though, not much to say,
She goes right on a-doin' things.
An' sometimes even laughs, and sings.
She says she don't feel extra well,
But then it's just a kind of spell,
She'll be all right tomorrow sure,
A good old sleep will be the cure.
An' pa he sniffs an' makes no kick,
For women folks is always sick,
An' Ma, she smiles, lets on she's glad . . .
When Ma is sick it ain't so bad.

—Unknown.

＊＞＞＜＜＊

Here's to those who love us,
    And here's to those who don't,
A smile for those who are willing to,
    And a tear for those who won't.

—Unknown.

HOMECOMING
HE

One hour more till my long day is through,
Gosh, I've had one million items to do!
But soon I'll be home and can leave all behind,
Never a worry or care in my mind;
I'll take a cool shower and good, soothing rub,
Coming all rosy and fresh from the tub;
And I'll sit in my den with my pipe and a book,
Shut up alone in my own cosy nook,
With my feet just as high as a guy's feet can go,
And my shoes and my socks in an untidy row . . .
Oh, to peel off my coat and my belt and my vest,
Jump on the sofa and just—simply—rest.

SHE

One hour more and my man'll be home
From the city's great marts and her vast honeycomb.
Then I'll get him to put on his old working clothes,
And sprinkle the lawn with the spray and the hose,
And rake up the yard of last winter's dead leaves,
And clean out the drain pipe that leaks from the eaves;
Then I'll ask him to hang up Aunt Belle's picture frame,
And teach little Junior to play his new game;
Then help with the supper—the table's not set—
And find out what's making the kitchen floor wet,
And set a fresh trap where those horrid mice lurk—
One hour more till he comes home to work!
                                        —Unknown.

FATHER

He was not the sort of father that you read about in
    books;
He wasn't long on language and he wasn't strong on looks.
He was not the sort of father that you hear about in
    plays . . .

He was just a human father, sort of quiet in his ways.
Just a sort of family father, fairly sound in wind and limb,
Always ready at the word and not a nasty trick or whim,
Seldom off his feed and never had to be turned out to
    graze,
Safe for any child to drive and broke to harness forty
    ways!
Steady at the bit was father; found a lot of fun in
    working;
Threw his weight against the collar; seemed to have no
    time for shirking.
Used to smile and say the feed-bin kept him steady on
    the track;
Safe to leave him without hitching; he'd be there when
    you came back.
No; he never balked at working, but when he was
    through it once,
Right down to the grass was father, with the children
    doing stunts.
Everyone would pile upon him and he'd welcome all the
    pack,
But I'm wondering, after playtime, did we stay there
    . . . on his back?
Wasn't strong on dissipation; said his "gambol on the
    green"
Was to fill the platter quicker than the kids could lick
    it clean,
And the next best game he knew of was an equal one to
    beat;
It was keeping leather covers up to the supply of feet!
Mind! his tailor never told him, when his Sunday coat
    was fitted,
That his wings necessitated wearing shoulders loose or
    slitted,
And he wasn't any martyr; said that life and love were good
And no man deserved his dinner if he wouldn't split the
    wood.

Always on the job was father, plugging quiet-like and
  strong,
Never making any noise, but helping all his little world
  along;
And to think . . . Lord! ain't it funny you can see
  things years and years
And you never knew they've been there, till your eyes
  are blind with tears!
Quit his job one day and left us, smiling as he went away;
Eulogy seems all so foolish; what can anybody say?
Seemed like even in his leaving he was saving someone
  bother
For the one word in the granite which is over him is . . .
  Father.

—Edmund Vance Cooke.

THE READING MOTHER

I had a Mother who read to me
Sagas of pirates who scoured the sea,
Cutlasses clenched in their yellow teeth,
"Blackbirds" stowed in the hold beneath.

I had a Mother who read me lays
Of ancient and gallant and golden days;
Stories of Marmion and Ivanhoe,
Which every boy has a right to know.

I had a Mother who read me tales
Of Celert the hound of the hills of Wales,
True to his trust till his tragic death,
Faithfulness blent with his final breath.

I had a Mother who read me the things
That wholesome life to the boy heart brings—
Stories that stir with an upward touch,
Oh, that each mother of boys were such!

You may have tangible wealth untold;
Caskets of jewels and coffers of gold.
Richer than I you can never be—
I had a Mother who read to me.
—Strickland Gillilan.

THIS WORLD

This world that we're a-livin' in
Is mighty hard to beat;
You git a thorn with every rose,
But *ain't* the roses *sweet!*
—Frank L. Stanton.

WHO LOVES THE RAIN

Who loves the rain
And loves his home,
And looks on life with quiet eyes,
Him will I follow through the storm;
And at his hearth-fire keep me warm;
Nor hell nor heaven shall that soul surprise,
Who loves the rain,
And loves his home,
And looks on life with quiet eyes.
—Frances Shaw.

HOME JOYS

Home joys are known in simple things,
In friends that share a cup of tea,
In books that waken old, old dreams
And songs that stir the memory.
—Rachel Ann Neiswender.

->>><<<-

Here's to wives and sweethearts!
May they never, never meet.
—Unknown.

JEST A WEARYIN' FER YOU

Jest a wearyin' fer you—
All the time a feelin' blue;
Wishin' for you—wonderin' when
You'll be comin' home again;
Restless—don't know what to do—
    Jest a wearyin' for you!

Room's so lonesome, with your chair,
Empty by the fireplace there,
Jest can't stand the sight of it!
Go outdoors and roam a bit;
But the woods is lonesome too,
    Jest a wearyin' fer you.

Mornin' comes, the birds awake
(Them that sung so fer your sake),
But there's sadness in the notes
That come trillin' from their throats!
Seem to feel your absence too—
    Jest a wearyin' fer you.

Evenin' comes; I miss you more
When the dark is in the door;
'Pears jest like you orter be
There to open it fer me!
Latch goes tinklin'—thrills me through,
    Sets me wearyin' fer you!

Jest a wearyin' fer you—
All the time a-feelin' blue!
Wishin' fer you—wonderin' when
You'll be comin' home again;
Restless—don't know what to do—
    Jest a wearyin' fer you!
                    —Frank L. Stanton.

SIMPLE THINGS

Give me the simple things close to my home,
  The things that are familiar, old and dear,
I do not have to wander far, or roam
  The Seven Seas—when I have splendour here.

Give me a crackling flame upon the grate
  And the warm smell of bread upon the fire.
I do not have to ride abroad in state
  To find the very core of heart's desire.

A shining tea pot—friendly hands to pour
  And jam that smells of grapes from our own vine.
Could any noble king desire more?
  I am a king myself, for these are mine.

Let those who will seek promised lands afar,
  For treasures so remote I shed no tear.
Why should I strive to reach a distant star
  When heaven with all its beauty is right here?
                                        —Dorothy Day.

->>-<<-

God made the world—and rested,
God made man—and rested,
Then God made woman,
Since then, neither God nor man has rested.
                                        —Unknown.

->>-<<-

Here's to woman, the sweetheart, the wife,
  The delight of our firesides by night and by day,
Who never does anything wrong in her life,
  Except when permitted to have her own way.
                                        —Fitz-Greene Halleck.

THE FIRE TENDERS

Women through the years have stood
　　Watch above a flame,
Keeping it a glowing thing
　　For the ones who came
Tired, hungry, when the night
Marked a kitchen's warm, red light.

Nothing lovelier, I think,
　　Than a woman's face,
Calmly bent above a fire.
　　As with quiet grace
She moves clean, deft hands to make
Food more wholesome for Love's sake.

Something great and beautiful
In her simple art—
Something to delight the mind,
The drip of rain on the roof and you in my thought
And no miracle at all.
　　　　　　　　　—Geoffrey Phibbs.

→⟩⟩⟨⟨←

We don't hope for a home on the shore by the sea,
　　Nor a hut at the end of a lane,
We don't want a villa, on a beach at Manila,
　　Nor hope for a castle in Spain.

We live in a flat, on the alley at that,
　　The windows are not very tall,
The kitchen is tiny, the gas stove's all shiny
　　And the parlor is awfully small.
But what do we care, we're the happiest pair,
　　We'd be happy with life in a hall,
Come see us some night, and you'll see that I'm right
　　We live for each other, that's all.
　　　　　　　　　—Unknown.

TRAIL END

A trail end, a cabin, a bit of blue sea!
These are the things that mean heaven to me!
And what does it matter, how humble, how far,
Just so I may find them, wherever they are.

A cabin that nestles against a round hill
Where mocking birds whistle and bees drone until
The honey-sweet air is a medley of song,
And crickets are fiddling the merry night long!

A bit of blue sea, and the tang of its salt,
A spar and a star in the heavenly vault.
What more can I ask, save an old song or two,
And a trail end that leads in the gloaming to you!
—Cristel Hastings.

SUN-DOWN SONG

There's a shabby little shanty leaning tipsy on a hill
  With an early lighted lamp already blinking;
There's a fresh and starchy lady waiting on the clean
    door sill;
  And, looking on the fields, the lady's thinking:

"He has ploughed the live-long day and he has sweated
    in the sun;
  Soon my cool and eager kiss he will be taking;
And when all his chores are finished and the feeding has
    been done
  He shall have the luscious pie I have been baking.

"O he may be just a plowman and go plodding through
    his days;
  He may toil and struggle through the toughest weather;
In his shack he's always lord of all the region he surveys;
  In his shack a lord and lady live together!"
—Janie Smith Rhyne.

YOUTH

I shall remember then,
At twilight-time or in the hush of dawn,
Or yet, mayhap, when on a straying wind
The scent of lilac comes, or when
Some strain of music startles and is gone.
Old dreams, old roses, all so far behind,
Blossoms and birds and ancient shadow-trees,
Whispers at sunset, the low hum of bees,
And sheep that graze beneath a summer sun,
Will they too, come, they who in yesteryear
Walked the same paths and in the first of spring;
And shall I hear
Their distant voices murmuring.

I shall remember then
When youth is done,
With the dim years grown gray;
And I shall wonder what it is that ends,
And why they seem so very far away . . .
Old dreams, old roses . . . old friends.
—Thomas S. Jones, Jr.

THE HOUSE BY THE SIDE OF THE ROAD

There are hermit souls that live withdrawn
   In the peace of their self-content;
There are souls, like stars, that dwell apart,
   In a fellowless firmament;
There are pioneer souls that blaze their paths
   Where highways never ran;—
But let me live by the side of the road
   And be a friend to man.

Let me live in a house by the side of the road,
   Where the race of men go by—

The men who are good and the men who are bad,
   As good and as bad as I.
I would not sit in the scorner's seat,
   Or hurl the cynic's ban;—
Let me live in the house by the side of the road
   And be a friend to man.

I see from my house by the side of the road,
   By the side of the highway of life,
The men who press with the ardor of hope,
   The men who are faint with the strife.
But I turn not away from their smiles nor their tears—
   Both parts of an infinite plan;—
Let me live in my house by the side of the road
   And be a friend to man.

I know there are brook-gladdened meadows ahead
   And mountains of wearisome height;
And the road passes on through the long afternoon
   And stretches away to the night.
But still I rejoice when the travelers rejoice,
   And weep with the strangers that moan,
Nor live in my house by the side of the road
   Like a man who dwells alone.

Let me live in my house by the side of the road
   Where the race of men go by—
They are good, they are bad, they are weak, they are
     strong,
   Wise, foolish—so am I.
Then why should I sit in the scorner's seat
   Or hurl the cynic's ban?—
Let me live in my house by the side of the road
   And be a friend to man.

                 —Samuel Walter Foss.

A PRETTY GOOD WORLD

Pretty good world if you take it all round—
   Pretty good world, good people!
Better be on than under the ground—
   Pretty good world, good people!
Better be here where the skies are as blue
As the eyes of your sweetheart a-smilin' at you—
Better than lyin' 'neath daisies and dew—
   Pretty good world, good people!

Pretty good world with its hopes and its fears—
   Pretty good world, good people!
Sun twinkles bright through the rain of its tears—
   Pretty good world, good people!
Better be here, in the pathway you know—
Where the thorn's in the garden where sweet roses grow,
Than to rest where you feel not the fall o' the snow—
   Pretty good world, good people!

Pretty good world! Let us sing it that way—
   Pretty good world, good people!
Make up your mind that you're in it to stay—
   At least for a season, good people!
Pretty good world, with its dark and its bright—
Pretty good world, with its love and its light;
Sing it that way till you whisper, "Good-night"!—
   Pretty good world, good people!
              —Frank L. Stanton.

4. TO MESS

To Mess

->>*<<-

THE RASPBERRY TREE

When I and the universe disagree,
I go and sit by the Raspberry Tree;
Under the ripe red raspberry rows
I lie on my back and wiggle my toes,
And listen for hours to the song in G
That the cuckoo sings
In the Raspberry Tree.

It isn't your fault (the cuckoo sings)
That people are people, and things are things,
That wheat and barley are cheaper than chaff,
And two times two is three and a half;
It isn't your fault that swans are geese
And dreams are sold for a dime apiece;
It isn't your fault
And it isn't your loss
That a stitch in time will gather no moss.

When the morning stars sing a bit off key,
I sit out under the Raspberry Tree;
The ripe red raspberries grow in tiers,
I close my eyes and wiggle my ears,
And I spend the whole of the afternoon
While the cuckoo sings me a ragtime tune.

What if you tried (is the cuckoo's song)
To fix whatever is going wrong?
The world is wide and the ocean's deep,
And you should worry and miss your sleep!

Losing your shirt is the least of ills—
Think what it saves in laundry bills!
Break your heart and it won't be fun,
But put it together and see it run!
It can't be helped,
But it can be mended—
Early to bed is soonest ended.

To be, says Hamlet, or not to be,
But I sit under my Raspberry Tree;
Thinking thoughts that are silly and kind,
I lie on my back and wiggle my mind,
With my soul attuned to the song in G
That the cuckoo sings
In the Raspberry Tree.

—Stoddard King.

THE HEIGHT OF THE RIDICULOUS

I wrote some lines once on a time
    In wondrous merry mood,
And thought, as usual, men would say
    They were exceedingly good.

They were so queer, so very queer,
    I laughed as I would die;
Albeit, in the general way,
    A sober man am I.

I called my servant, and he came;
    How kind it was of him,
To mind a slender man like me,
    He of the mighty limb!

"These to the printer," I exclaimed,
    And, in my humorous way,
I added (as a trifling jest),
    "There'll be the devil to pay."

He took the paper, and I watched,
  And saw him peep within;
At the first line he read, his face
  Was all upon the grin.

He read the next; the grin grew broad,
  And shot from ear to ear;
He read the third; a chuckling noise
  I now began to hear.

The fourth; he broke into a roar;
  The fifth; his waistband split;
The sixth; he burst five buttons off,
  And tumbled in a fit.

Ten days and nights, with sleepless eye,
  I watched that wretched man,
And since, I never dare to write
  As funny as I can.
                            —Oliver Wendell Holmes.

TENDER-HEARTEDNESS

Billie, in one of his nice new sashes,
Fell in the fire and was burnt to ashes;
Now, although the room grows chilly,
I haven't the heart to poke poor Billie.
                            —Colonel D. Streamer.

THE PRAYER OF CYRUS BROWN

"The proper way for a man to pray,"
  Said Deacon Lemuel Keyes,
"And the only proper attitude
  Is down upon his knees."

"No, I should say the way to pray,"
  Said Rev. Doctor Wise,

"Is standing straight with outstretched arms
   And rapt and upturned eyes."

"Oh, no, no, no," said Elder Slow,
   "Such posture is too proud:
A man should pray with eyes fast closed
   And head contritely bowed."

"It seems to me his hands should be
   Austerely clasped in front,
With both thumbs pointing toward the ground,"
   Said Rev. Doctor Blunt.

"Las' year I fell in Hodgkin's well
   Head first," said Cyrus Brown,
"With both my heels a-stickin' up,
   My head a-pinting down;

"An' I made a prayer right then an' there—
   Best prayer I ever said,
The prayingest prayer I ever prayed,
   A-standing on my head."
                              —Samuel Walter Foss.

PREHISTORIC SMITH

Quaternary Epoch—Post-Pliocene Period

A man sat on a rock and sought
   Refreshment from his thumb;
A dinotherium wandered by
   And scared him some.

His name was Smith. The kind of rock
   He sat upon was shale.
One feature quite distinguished him—
   He had a tail.

The danger past, he fell into
    A revery austere;
While with his tail he whisked a fly
    From off his ear.

"Mankind deteriorates," he said,
    "Grows weak and incomplete;
And each new generation seems
    Yet more effete.

"Nature abhors imperfect work,
    And on it lays her ban;
And all creation must despise
    A tailless man.

"But fashion's dictates rule supreme,
    Ignoring common sense;
And fashion says, to dock your tail
    Is just immense.

"And children now come in the world
    With half a tail or less;
Too stumpy to convey a thought,
    And meaningless.

"It kills expression. How can one
    Set forth, in words that drag,
The best emotions of the soul,
    Without a wag?"

Sadly he mused upon the world,
    Its follies and its woes;
Then wiped the moisture from his eyes,
    And blew his nose.

But clothed in earrings, Mrs. Smith
  Came wandering down the dale;
And, smiling, Mr. Smith arose,
  And wagged his tail.
                    —David Law Proudfit.

UNSATISFIED YEARNING

Down in the silent hallway
  Scampers the dog about,
And whines and barks and scratches,
  In order to get out.

Once in the glittering starlight,
  He straightway doth begin
To set up a doleful howling
  In order to get in!
                    —R. K. Munkittrick.

A fish seems very sad to me,
  No matter what its trouble;
It opens up its mouth to moan
  And just emits—a bubble.
                    —Rebecca McCann.

DISCOVERY

A caterpillar squirmed
  Up to a lettuce leaf
And panted at the top
  In woolly-worm relief.

On pancake world of green
  And dizzy depths of brown
It gaped: "Now I've seen everything!"
  And slowly slithered down.
                    —Dorothy Sigmund.

ZOOLOGICAL OBSERVATION

The hyena does not hunt for game.
She appeases her hunger with the carcasses
Of animals killed by the daring.

Some women find satisfaction
In capturing other women's husbands . . .
—Rosa Zagnoni Marinoni.

TO FISH

You strange, astonished-looking, angle-faced,
  Dreary-mouthed, gaping wretches of the sea,
  Gulping salt-water everlastingly,
Cold-blooded, though with red your blood be graced,
And mute, though dwellers in the roaring waste;
  And you, all shapes beside, that fishy be,—
  Some round, some flat, some long, all devilry,
Legless, unloving, infamously chaste:—

O scaly, slippery, wet, swift, staring wights,
  What is't ye do? what life lead? eh, dull goggles?
How do ye vary your vile days and nights?
  How pass your Sundays? Are ye still but joggles
In ceaseless wash? Still nought but gapes, and bites,
  And drinks, and stares, diversified with boggles?
—Leigh Hunt.

PARABLE FOR A CERTAIN VIRGIN

Oh, ponder, friend, the porcupine;
  Refresh your recollection,
And sit a moment, to define
  His means of self-protection.

How truly fortified is he!
  Where is the beast his double

In forethought of emergency
    And readiness for trouble?

Recall his figure, and his shade—
    How deftly planned and clearly
For slithering through the dappled glade
    Unseen, or pretty nearly.

Yet should an alien eye discern
    His presence in the woodland,
How little has he left to learn
    Of self-defense! My good land!

For he can run, as swift as sound,
    To where his goose may hang high;
Or thrust his head against the ground
    And tunnel half to Shanghai;

Or he can climb the dizziest bough—
    Unhesitant, mechanic—
And, resting, dash from off his brow
    The bitter beads of panic;

Or should pursuers press him hot,
    One scarcely needs to mention
His quick and cruel barbs, that got
    Shakespearean attention;

Or driven to his final ditch,
    To his extremest thicket,
He'll fight with claws and molars (which
    Is not considered cricket).

How amply armored, he, to fend
    The fear of chase that haunts him!
How well prepared our little friend!—
    And who the devil wants him?
                 —Dorothy Parker.

THE FROG

What a wonderful bird the frog are—
When he stand he sit almost
When he hops, he fly almost
He ain't got no sense hardly
He ain't got no tail hardly either
When he sit, he sit on what he ain't got almost!

—Unknown.

PERILS OF THINKING

A centipede was happy quite,
   Until a frog in fun
Said, "Pray, which leg comes after which?"
This raised her mind to such a pitch,
She lay distracted in the ditch
   Considering how to run.   —Unknown.

MAGGIE'S FINISH

Inscription on a monument in France which marks the last resting place of an Army mule:

In memory of Maggie, who in her time kicked two colonels, four majors, 10 captains, 24 lieutenants, 42 sergeants, 432 other ranks, and one Mills bomb.

—Unknown.

THE LACQUER LIQUOR LOCKER

Now once upon a time the King of Astrakhan, at that,
Was sitting on his throne because his throne was where
  he sat;
And comfortably beside him, and magnificently stocked,
Was a lacquer liquor locker which a liquor lackey locked.

"My boy," the King would often say with granulate
  voice,
"I think the 1640 is particularly choice."

The boy would understand and so, endeavoring to please,
He'd try his luck at fitting several likely locker keys.

The King was always much annoyed because of this
    delay:
"See here, my lad, you've got to throw those other keys
    away."
"This minute, Sire?" "This minute, sir!" And with a pox
    that pocked,
He cursed the keys which didn't keep his liquor locker
    locked.

The lackey did as he was bid. Alackalasalack!
He threw them all so far away that no one threw them
    back.
A silly throw, as I can show, for he was simply shocked
To find he lacked the very one that left the liquor locked.
                                            —David McCord.

EVE

He was a god to her,
    Powerful, kindly.
She would have died for him,
    Gladly and blindly.

Imagine the shock when she
    Found he was human—
And heard him, quite man-like,
    Blaming a woman!
                —Eleanor Stanley Lockwood.

SIDELINE OBSERVATION

There are lots of things
I can't see,
    but here's one thing that I know:
in the spring a young man's fancy
    and an old one's not so slow.
                —Kathryn Kay.

THE ROOKIE'S SONG

(As the folks at home imagine it)

O, I'm a gay Lothario
I'm wilder than old Pharaoh,
 I'm long on what is known as sex appeal;
I've got the ladies' numero,
They're after me where'er I go,
 I clinch 'em at the end of every reel.

I've flirted with a hundred belles
Of plain and ornamental smells,
 To the lovelight in their lamps I'm always wised;
I meet them and I say goodbye,
It's tough, but if a few should die
 I'm telling you I wouldn't be surprised!

I've petted 'em beneath the rose,
I've loved the dimpled Esquimoze,
 I've squoze the little maids of old Japan;
In Turkey and the Barbadoes,
From Afric sands to Russian snows,
 Unanimously, folks, I am the man!
     —Norman H. Crowell.

SMOKE RINGS

Bad Men want their women
To be like cigarettes,
Just so many, all slender and trim
In a case,
Waiting in a row
To be selected, set aflame, and
When their flame has died
Discarded.

More Fastidious Men
Prefer women like cigars.

These are more exclusive,
Look better and last longer;
If the brand is good,
They aren't given away.

Good Men treat women
Like pipes
And become more attached to them
The older they become!
When the flame is burnt out
They still look after them,
Knock them gently
(But lovingly)
And care for them always—
No man shares his pipe.

—Unknown.

UNHOLY DOZEN

I

A wicked book gathers no dust.

II

Once the butterfly
of Love
crawls into the cocoon
of Marriage,
it becomes a caterpillar.

III

If our heads were put up at auction
the bids of our best friends
would greatly disappoint us.

IV

Fire, earthquake and cyclones
destroy Houses,
but it takes a woman to destroy
a Home.

VII

Never tell a secret.
But if you must,
tell it to a recognized liar!
When he repeats it,
no one will believe him.

. . .

IX

Fame is an old forgotten well
surrounded by tall weeds.
Once in a while
men stumble into it
on their way to work.

. . .

XI

Do not feel sorry
for the wife who
goes through
her husband's pockets,
but rather for the one
who is afraid to.

—Rosa Zagnoni Marinoni.

AN EXCEPTION

"I'd trust my husband anywhere," she said;
"My faith in him is full, 'tis satisfied;
I know that all his thoughts are fair," she said—
"I know he'd put temptations all aside.

"I know that he is strong, sublime," she said;
"I know that all his love is mine, for e'er;
I'd trust my husband anywhere," she said—
"Unless a woman happened to be there."

—S. E. Kiser.

PATHOS PATERNAL

Why do people so seldom bother
To pity the plight of the expectant father
Who sits and chews his fingernails
And strains his ears for baby wails?
Oh, for a bed that he might lie on,
And meditate on Papa Dionne:
If only he had some way of knowing
To what extent the family's growing.
And what will it weigh and will it have feet,
Or will it resemble a pickled beet?
No, the local papers never tell
If "*Father* and child are doing well!"

—John M. Morris.

MY PIPE

My pipe is old
    And caked with soot;
My wife remarks:
    "How can you put
That horrid relic
    So unclean,
Inside your mouth?
    The nicotine
Is strong enough
    To stupefy
A Swedish plumber."
    I reply:

"This is the kind
    Of pipe I like:
I fill it full
    Of Happy Strike,
Of Barking Cat
    Or Cabman's Puff,

Or Brooklyn Bridge
 (That potent stuff)
Or Chaste Embraces,
 Knacker's Twists,
Old Honeycomb
 Or Niggerfist.

"I clamp my teeth
 Upon its stem—
It is my bliss,
 My diadem.
Whatever Fate
 May do to me,
This is my favorite
 B.
 B B.
For this dear pipe
 You feign to scorn
I smoked the night
 The boy was born."
     —Christopher Morley.

JABBERWOCKY

'Twas brillig, and the slithy toves
 Did gyre and gimble in the wabe;
All mimsy were the borogoves,
 And the mome raths outgrabe.

"Beware the Jabberwock, my son!
 The jaws that bite, the claws that catch!
Beware the Jubjub bird, and shun
 The frumious Bandersnatch!"

He took his vorpal sword in hand;
 Long time the manxome foe he sought—
So rested he by the Tumtum tree,
 And stood awhile in thought.

And, as in uffish thought he stood,
   The Jabberwock, with eyes of flame,
Came whiffling through the tulgey wood,
   And burbled as it came!

One, two! One, two! and through and through
   The vorpal blade went snicker-snack!
He left it dead, and with its head
   He went galumphing back.

"And hast thou slain the Jabberwock?
   Come to my arms, my beamish boy!
O frabjous day! Callooh, Callay!"
   He chortled in his joy.

'Twas brillig, and the slithy toves
   Did gyre and gimble in the wabe;
All mimsy were the borogoves,
   And the mome raths outgrabe.
                —Lewis Carroll.

SIR MURGATROYD AT SEBASTAPOOL

Sebastapool The Mangler was a wrestler known and
   feared
Wherever and whenever he professionally appeared.
He was just a blob of blubber with the contour of a barrel,
But every ounce was double-packed with petrifying peril!
His arms were thick as tree-trunks and his fists as big as
   pails,
And when he gripped a grappler what was left was
   "mere details."
Tho some there were who doubted what he had below his
   hat,
Sebastapool The Mangler was almighty on the mat
And none, whatever else they thought, had ever ques-
   tioned *that*.

Among the famous champions of whom epic tales are told,
Sir Murgatroyd The Murderer was something to behold!
A big, ferocious, bullet-headed, bellows-chested gent
With a locomotive chassis and a jaw of pure cement.
He was wicked, he was nasty, he was anything but nice,
And he seldom signed a challenger who thought about
 it twice.
But Sebastapool the Mangler, with a terrifying leer,
Roared, "*Who the hell is Murgatroyd*—the pretty little
 dear!
I'll crush him to a jelly and I'll spread him on the mat
And I'll eat 'em both together fer me vitamins and fat."

Now, gentlemen, I needn't say that "them was fightin'
 speeches,"
The kind that lead to sanctions and to diplomatic
 breaches.
They were not merely persiflage or idle talk or banter;
The challenge here was squarely meant and squarely met
 instanter.
Sir Murgatroyd was not the man to see his status
 dwindling;
He pounded on the table-top and smashed it into
 kindling;
And he hollered, "Why, the so-and-so! I'll pulverize his
 guts!"
To which Sebastapool replied, in perfect English, "*Nuts!*"

They met November twenty-third at Riverside Arena;
Gilhooley was the timer, and the referee, De Pinna.
A hundred thousand noses faced the roped and matted
 ring—
Celebrities and movie stars and all that sort of thing.
The Mangler and the Murderer were full of fight and bile;
They glowered at the camera men who crowded in the
 aisle;

They glowered at each other, too, and at the referee—
The sight was stark . . . or primitive . . . or savage
　　. . . or all three!

But Referee De Pinna was a fearless man, and stern;
There wasn't much about the game De Pinna had to
　　learn.
He was a scrawny little guy, as nervous as a cat,
But every second in the ring he knew where he was at.
You couldn't fool him on a foul or gyp him on a fall,
And when he said a man was down—why he was *down*—
　　that's all!

It was eight o'clock precisely that he bounded in the ring
And he raised a hand for silence with the grandeur of a
　　king.
He called the burly battlers to the center of the mat
And gave them their instructions in just thirty seconds
　　flat.
The Mangler and the Murderer, their eyes ablaze with
　　hate,
Shook hands, with him between 'em, at one minute after
　　eight.
A silence, short but ominous—a silence, then *the bell!*
They met like sizzling cannon balls exploded out of Hell.

Observers saw a burst of smoke from scorching cloth and
　　leather
And with a loud resounding grunt they wrapped them-
　　selves together!
Sebastapool and Murgatroyd were, arm and leg and
　　torso,
About as homogeneous as a meatball is—or more so.

It was no very easy task to get them both untangled—
The Mangler was half murdered and The Murderer half
　　mangled!

And no one knew exactly who between them was the
"*winnah*,"
For no one could find hide or hair of Referee De Pinna!

His mourners raised a handsome shaft recording the
disaster
Surmounted by a Dove of Peace in virgin alabaster.

Moral:

But two sides hath an argument, and who essays a third,
He winneth not, he loseth not—he only gets "*the bird*."
—Joseph S. Newman.

EX-VIRGIN'S LAMENT

Tonight Love is a smiling lad
with bright and shining eyes.
Ah, Love, why must it make me sad
to know I am so wise?
Tonight Love says, "Be mine once more!"
I close my eyes and curse,
Because—I've heard that song before—
I know the second verse!
—Kathryn Kay.

LET THE TOAST PASS

Here's to the maiden of bashful fifteen,
Here's to the widow of fifty:
Here's to the flaunting extravagant queen,
And here's to the housewife that's thrifty.

Let the toast pass! drink to the lass!
I'll warrant she'll prove an excuse for the glass.

Here's to the charmer whose dimples we prize,
Now to the maid who has none, sir;
Here's to the girl with a pair of blue eyes,
And here's to the nymph with but one, sir.

Here's to the maid with a bosom of snow,
    And to her that's as brown as a berry;
Here's to the wife, with a face full of woe,
    And now to the girl that is merry.

For let 'em be clumsy, or let 'em be slim,
    Young or ancient, I care not a feather;
So fill the pint bumper quite up to the brim,
So fill up your glasses, nay fill to the brim,
    And let us e'en toast em together.
        Let the toast pass! drink to the lass!
        I'll warrant she'll prove an excuse for the glass.
                            —Richard Brinsley Sheridan.

EPITAPH ON HIS WIFE

Here lies my wife: here let her lie!
Now she's at rest—and so am I.
                            —John Dryden.

ESSAY ON MAN

Man is what a woman marries.
Men have two feet, two hands, and sometimes two
wives, but never more than one collar button or one idea
at a time. Like Turkish cigarettes, men are all made of
the same material, the only difference is that some are
better disguised than others. Generally speaking, they
may be divided into three classes—husbands, bachelors,
and widowers. An eligible bachelor is a man of obstinacy
surrounded with suspicion. Husbands are of three varie-
ties—prize, surprise, and consolation prize. Making a
husband out of a man is one of the highest plastic arts
known to civilization. It requires science, sculpture,
and common sense, faith, hope, and charity—mostly
charity. It is a psychological marvel that a soft, fluffy,
tender, violet-scented, sweet thing like woman should
enjoy kissing a big awkward, stubbly-chinned, tobacco
and bay-rum-scented thing like man.

If you flatter a man, it frightens him to death, and if you don't you bore him to death. If you permit him to make love to you, he gets tired of you in the end, and if you don't, he gets tired of you in the beginning.

If you wear gay colors, rouge, and startling hats, he hesitates to take you out. If you wear a little brown toque and tailor-made suit, he takes you out and stares all evening at a woman in gay colors, rouge, and a startling hat.

If you are the clinging-vine type, he doubts whether you have a brain. If you are the modern type, an advanced and independent woman, he doubts whether you have a heart. If you are surly he longs for a bright mate, and if you are brilliant, he longs for a playmate. If you are popular with other men, he is jealous, and if you are not, he hesitates to marry a wallflower. If you please him, he seldom mentions it, but if you displease him, he never fails to tell you about it, especially if you are his wife.

That's all. —M. E. Perry.

ADVICE TO DAUGHTER

"Daughter," I said, "You have reached the age
    Where advice from your mother is needed.
I will take from the Book of Experience a page,
    And I want you to take it and heed it."

I quoted aloud as she paced the room—
    (Daughter has a wonderful carriage)
"It's all right to listen to love in bloom,
    But *run* if a man mentions marriage."

Now, daughter was always an obedient child,
    Coming really close to perfection,
But her calculations were somewhat wild—
    Daughter ran in the wrong direction!
                 —Lillian Taylor.

POEMS IN PRAISE OF PRACTICALLY NOTHING

I

You buy some flowers for your table;
You tend them tenderly as you're able;
You fetch them water from hither and thither—
What thanks do you get for it all? They wither.

    •   •   •   •

III

You buy yourself a new suit of clothes;
The care you give it, God only knows;
The material, of course, is the very *best* yet;
You get it pressed and pressed and *pressed* yet;
You keep it free from specks *so* tiny—
What thanks do you get? The pants get shiny.

    •   •   •

V

You leap out of bed; you start to get ready;
You dress and you dress till you feel unsteady;
Hours go by, and still you're busy
Putting on clothes, till your brain is dizzy.
Do you flinch? Do you quit? Do you go out naked?—
The least little button, you don't forsake it.
What thanks do you get? Well, for all this mess, yet
When night comes around, you've got to undress yet.

    •   •   •   •

VIII

You take a bath, and sit there bathing
In water cold, in water scathing;
You scrub till you're sans an epidermis,
And feel like a regular bathing Hermes.

You do not waste a single minute;
The tub shows how you worked while in it;
You dry, and do some honest rooting
For such remarkable abluting:—
Well, a day goes by, or ten, or thirty,
And what thanks do you get? You're just as dirty!

. . . .

IX

You meet a girl and you surrender;
Though God knows why, you're kind and tender;
You're husband, lover, sister, brother,
Companion, banker, father, mother;
You try your best to be worthy of her;
You make mistakes, but she knows you love her;
You're hers completely, and you show it:
And what thanks do you get? The gate—I know it!

X

You're a good girl; you're gray with virtue;
The very thought of a misstep hurts you;
You know that honor must be hoarded
Against the day when it is rewarded;
You see a girl who's all men's vassal,
Marry a duke in his own castle;
You see another, who can't say, "No, sir,"
Capture, at least, a wholesale grocer:—
But you never let your thoughts grow sordid:
You know in your heart you'll be rewarded.
Well, the years go by, like queens and roses,
The way they did in the time of Moses,
And what do you get? False teeth, a doorman,
A complex, or assistant foreman!
                                        —Samuel Hoffenstein.

꘎꘎꘎

My grandpa notes the world's worn cogs
And says we're going to the dogs.
His granddad in his house of logs
Swore things were going to the dogs.
His dad among the Flemish bogs
Vowed things were going to the dogs.
The caveman in his queer skin togs
Said things were going to the dogs.
But this is what I wish to state—
The dogs have had an awful wait.

—Unknown.

ON THE ANTIQUITY OF MICROBES

Adam
Had 'em.

—Strickland Gillilan.

FRIENDS

Some are true;
Others are not.
They either love you,
Or what you've got.

—Bea Myers.

HAND HIM A HALO!

Perhaps *your* bread on *both* sides has been buttered!
Perhaps *your* cake is eaten and you *have* it, too!
Perhaps *all* pearls have been the words *you've* uttered!
Perhaps *you've* never bitten *more* than you can chew!

Who gives a rap
For such a chap?

—Addison H. Hallock.

CROMEK SPEAKS

I always take my judgment from a fool
Because his judgment is so very cool;
Not prejudiced by feelings great or small.
Amiable state! He cannot feel at all.

—William Blake.

LINES (2) ON THE QUESTIONABLE IMPORTANCE OF THE INDIVIDUAL

I . . .
Why?

—Unknown.

→»×«←

I wish I were a little rock
A-sittin' on a hill
A-doin' nothin' all day long,
—Just a-settin' still.
I wouldn't eat,
I wouldn't sleep,
I wouldn't even wash,
I'd just sit still,
A thousand years,
And rest myself "by Gosh!"

—Unknown.

SPRINGTIME IS NO LADY

Springtime is no lady;
  I'll tell you how I know;
Last night I saw her walking
  Down a japonica row.
At the bottom of the garden
  She paused to smooth her hair
And with a snowdrop powdered her nose
  With a most impeccable air.

But springtime is no lady:
  And O, it's I who know,
She and the wind, they held a tryst
  Down where the blue flags grow.
They stumbled thru the marsh land
  They tripped from hill to hill
They wandered in the meadow
  And the gay wind had his will.

I tell you, Spring's no lady!
  This is how I know:
Today blue flags are purple
  The meadow grasses grow
The wind is high and lusty
  It's plain he's had his way
And Spring's a maid no longer:
  The hills are large with May!
                    —Laurie Parkinson.

LOVE CARES NOT FOR NAMES

Her name was only Maggie, and his was merely John,
  And she was someone's nursemaid, and he worked by
    the day;
John wore no braided jacket with medals pinned thereon,
  And Maggie wasn't gifted in any special way.

But John made love to Maggie, and Maggie's heart was
    glad,
  And this I tell you frankly, and beg you to believe:
Their case was as romantic as if the lover had
  Been christened Montmorency, and his loved one
    Genevieve.
                    —S. E. Kiser.

->>><<<-

Her lips were burning close, and a divine
Clear light shone in her eyes, that seemed to say
That which her tongue might not: "Yes, love mine,
                You may."
Methought, I'll seize the occasion ere it slips;
And swiftly as her luring glances spoke
I stopped to touch the heaven of her lips—
                And woke!
                                —Unknown.

POPPING CORN

And there they sat, a-pop'n corn,
    John Styles and Susan Cutter—
John Styles as fat as any ox,
    And Susan fat as butter.

And there they sat and shelled the corn,
    And raked and stirred the fire
And talked of different kinds of corn
    And hitched their chairs up nigher.

Then Susan she the popper shook
    Then John shook the popper,
Till both their faces grew as red
    As saucepans made of copper.

And then they shelled, and popped, and ate,
    All kinds of fun-a-poking,
While he he-hawed at her remarks,
    And she laughed at his joking.

And still they popped, and still they ate—
    John's mouth was like a hopper—
And stirred the fire and sprinkled salt,
    And shook and shook the popper.

The clock struck nine—the clock struck ten,
  And still the corn kept popping;
It struck eleven, and then struck twelve,
  And still no signs of stopping.

And John he ate, and Sue she thought—
  The corn did pop and patter—
Till John cried out, "The corn's a-fire!
  Why, Susan, what's the matter?"

Said she, "John Styles, it's one o'clock:
  You'll die of indigestion;
I'm sick of all this popping corn—
  Why don't you pop the question?"
                                    —Unknown.

WHY DON'T THE MEN PROPOSE?

Why don't the men propose, mamma?
  Why don't the men propose?
Each seems just coming to the point,
  And then away he goes!
It is no fault of yours, mamma,
  That everybody knows;
You fete the finest men in town,
  Yet, oh! they don't propose!

I'm sure I've done my best, mamma,
  To make a proper match;
For coronets and eldest sons
  I'm ever on the watch;
I've hopes when some distingué beau
  A glance upon me throws;
But though he'll dance, and smile, and flirt,
  Alas! he won't propose!

I've tried to win by languishing
    And dressing like a blue;
I've bought big books and talked of them
    As if I'd read them through!
With hair cropped like a man, I've felt
    The heads of all the beaux;
But Spurzheim would not touch their hearts,
    And, oh! they won't propose!

I threw aside the books, and thought
    That ignorance was bliss;
I felt convinced that men preferred
    A simple sort of miss;
And so I lisped out naught beyond
    Plain "yesses" and plain "noes,"
And wore a sweet, unmeaning smile;
    Yet, oh! they won't propose!

Last night at Lady Ramble's rout,
    I heard Sir Harry Gale
Exclaim, "Now I propose again;"
    I started turning pale;
I really thought my time was come,
    I blushed like any rose;
But oh! I found 'twas only at
    Ecarte he'd propose!

And what is to be done, mamma?
    Oh, what is to be done?
I really have no time to lose,
    For I am thirty-one:
At balls I am too often left
    Where spinsters sit in rows;
Why don't the men propose, mamma?
    Why don't the men propose?
                    —Thomas Haynes Bailey.

ANY ONE WILL DO

A maiden once, of certain age,
To catch a husband did engage;
But, having passed the prime of life
In striving to become a wife
Without success, she thought it time
To mend the follies of her prime.

Departing from the usual courses
Of paint and such like resources,
With all her might this ancient maid
Beneath an oak tree knelt and prayed;
Unconscious that a grave old owl
Was perched above—the mousing fowl!

"Oh, give! a husband give!" she cried,
"While I may yet become a bride;
Soon will my day of grace be o'er,
And then, like many maids before,
I'll die without an early love,
And none to meet me there above!

"Oh, 'tis a fate too hard to bear!
Then answer this my humble prayer,
And oh, a husband give to me!"
Just then the owl from out the tree,
In deep bass tones cried, "Who-who-who!"
"Who, Lord? and dost thou ask me who?
Why, any one, good Lord, will do."

—Unknown.

THE COURTIN'

God makes sech nights, all white an' still
    Fur'z you can look or listen,
Moonshine an' snow on field an' hill,
    All silence an' all glisten.

Zekle crep' up quite unbeknown
    An' peeked in thru' the winder,
An' there sot Huldy all alone,
    'ith no one nigh to hender.

A fireplace filled the room's one side,
    With half a cord o' wood in—
There warn't no stoves (tell comfort died)
    To bake ye to a puddin'.

The very room, coz she was in,
    Seemed warm f'om floor to ceilin',
An' she looked full ez rosy agin
    Ez the apples she was peelin'.

      .   .   .   .

He was six foot o' man, A 1,
    Clear grit an' human natur';
None couldn't quicker pitch a ton,
    Nor dror a furrer straighter.

He'd sparked it with full twenty gals,
    He'd squired 'em, danced 'em, druv 'em,
Fust this one, an' then thet, by spells—
    All is, he couldn't love 'em.

But long o' her his veins 'ould run
    All crinkly like curled maple,
The side she breshed felt full o' sun
    Ez a south slope in Ap'il.

She thought no v'ice hed sech a swing
    Ez his'n in the choir;
My! when he made Ole Hundred ring,
    She knowed the Lord was nigher.

An' she'd blush scarlit, right in prayer,
   When her new meetin'-bunnet
Felt somehow thru' its crown a pair
   O' blue eyes sot upon it.

Thet night, I tell ye, she looked *some!*
   She seemed to've gut a new soul,
For she felt sartin-sure he'd come,
   Down to her very shoe-sole.

She heered a foot, an' knowed it tu,
   A-raspin' on the scraper,—
All ways to once her feelin's flew
   Like sparks in burnt-up paper.

He kin' o' l'itered on the mat,
   Some doubtfle o' the sekle,
His heart kep' goin' pitty-pat,
   But hern went pity Zekle.

An' yit she gin her cheer a jerk
   Ez though she wished him furder,
An' on her apples kep' to work,
   Parin' away like murder.

"You want to see my Pa, I s'pose?"
   "Wal . . . no . . . I come dasignin'"—
"To see my Ma? She's sprinklin' clo'es
   Agin to-morrer's i'nin'."

To say why gals acts so or so,
   Or don't, 'ould be presumin';
Mebby to mean *yes* an' say *no*
   Comes nateral to women.

He stood a spell on one foot fust,
　Then stood a spell on t'other,
An' on which one he felt the wust
　He couldn't ha' told ye nuther.

Says he, "I'd better call ag'in";
　Says she, "Think likely, Mister";
Thet last word pricked him like a pin,
　An' . . . . Wal, he up an' kissed her.

When Ma bimeby upon 'em slips,
　Huldy sot pale ez ashes,
All kinda smily roun' the lips
　An teary roun' the lashes.

For she was jes' the quiet kind
　Whose naturs never vary,
Like streams that keep a summer mind
　Snow-hid in Jenooary.

The blood clost roun' her heart felt glued
　Too tight for all expressin',
Tell mother see how metters stood
　And gin 'em both her blessin'.

Then her red come back like the tide
　Down to the Bay o' Fundy,
An' all I know is they was cried
　In meetin' come nex' Sunday.
　　　　　　　　—James Russell Lowell.

>>><<<

Let us have wine and women, mirth and laughter—
Sermons and soda water the day after.
　　　　　　　　—Lord Byron.

As I walked through the grove on a midsummer eve
Misty, shimmering things in the air I perceive.
In tones low and sweet they forbid me to roam
And oft the mosquitoes have driven me home,
                                        —Unknown.

She laid a pale and still white form
    Beside the others there,
And then her anguished piercing shrieks
    Rang through the silent air.

With still another mournful wail
    She turned upon one leg.
Tomorrow she'll come back again
    And lay another egg.

                                        —Unknown.

I like to hear the rooster crow,
He's like so many men I know,
Who roar and rant and rave and shout
And beat their manly chests, without
A darn thing to brag about.

                                        —Unknown.

Here's to you two and to we two too;
    If you love we two,
    As we love you two,
    Then here's to we four:
But if you don't love we two
    As we two love you two,
    Then here's to we two
    And no more.

                                        —Unknown.

5. TO ARMS

To Arms

>>>)<<<

DON JUAN

Man's love is of man's life a thing apart,
   'Tis woman's whole existence; man may range
The court, camp, church, the vessel, and the mart,
   Sword, gown, gain, glory, offer in exchange
Pride, fame, ambition, to fill up his heart,
   And few there are whom these cannot estrange;
Men have all these resources, we but one,
To love again, and be again undone.
                     —Lord Byron.

ON A GIRDLE

That which her slender waist confined
Shall now my joyful temples bind:
No monarch but would give his crown
His arms might do what this has done.

It was my heaven's extremest sphere,
The pale which held that lovely dear:
My joy, my grief, my hope, my love,
Did all within this circle move.

A narrow compass! and yet there
Dwelt all that's good, and all that's fair:
Give me but what this riband bound,
Take all the rest the sun goes round.
                     —Edmund Waller.

THE TIME I'VE LOST IN WOOING

The time I've lost in wooing,
In watching and pursuing
  The light that lies
  In woman's eyes
Has been my heart's undoing.
Tho' Wisdom oft has sought me,
I scorn'd the love she brought me,
  My only books
  Were woman's looks
And folly's all they've taught me.

. . . . .

And are those follies going?
And is my proud heart growing
  Too cold or wise
  For brilliant eyes
Again to set it glowing?
No—vain, alas! th' endeavor
From bonds so sweet to sever;—
  Poor Wisdom's chance
  Against a glance
Is now as weak as ever.

—Thomas Moore.

TO THE VIRGINS

Gather ye rosebuds while ye may,
  Old Time is still a-flying:
And this same flower that smiles to-day
  To-morrow will be dying.

The glorious lamp of heaven, the sun,
  The higher he's a-getting,
The sooner will his race be run,
  And nearer he's to setting.

That age is best which is the first,
　When youth and blood are warmer;
But being spent, the worse, and worst
　Times still succeed the former.

Then be not coy, but use your time,
　And while ye may, go marry:
For having lost but once your prime,
　You may for ever tarry.
　　　　　　　　　—Robert Herrick.

LOVE SONNETS OF A LIGHT-MINDED LYRIST

Addressing you, my lord, in stately rhyme
　Is not the easy task it might have been
When poets walked among the springing thyme
　And sentiment was not a mortal sin.
I cannot sing you blossoms on the bough
　Nor yet the wavelets bubbling on the shore;
I dare not weave a chaplet for your brow
　Unless I would be thought a deadly bore;
A dainty ballad bright with birds and bees
　Would spell eternal ruin to my fame;
We are concerned with truer things than these
　Who know that life is death and honor shame
And all good songs are songs of dissappointment,
Of badly rifted lutes, of flies in ointment.

And seeing I am no apothecary
　And no great friend to ointment nor to flies,
And have had little wit enough to marry
　Where love is light and generous and wise,
And I am stranger to the knitted brow,
　The heaving bosom's pain, the muttered curse,
The sick and lurching heart, the broken vow,
　How much can be expected of my verse?

What would you have, my lord, who need no tether,
    Who fill my days with merriment and books,
Who keep your execrations for the weather,
    And for your garden all your passionate looks?
Surely no sight can stir the Muses less
Than two calm heads suspended over chess.

I love you; make the most of it; 'tis true,
    What would you have me say? That I am blind,
Deaf, dumb, and crippled out of sight of you,
    And, seeing you, have nothing else in mind?
That I would rather die than quit your side,
    That I do die, in sooth, a little death
Each time you leave me; that my only pride
    Is loving you, your life my only breath?
Ah, good my lord, if that you dream of such
    Extravagance, you dream of wordy waste;
I love you, and I love you very much;
    Exaggerate it to your personal taste,
And wonder—being masculine and human—
Why simple truth should so alarm a woman.

Man's love is of man's life a thing apart,
    'Tis woman's whole existence . . . If you please,
Far be it from my still ungrudging heart
    To rob you of such purring words as these.
Even Lord Byron—may his rest be sound!—
    Lies for this deed beneath no curse of mine;
He was a man, and spoke in nature bound
    With innocence less human than divine.
Quote him again, I beg, and yet once more,
    So long as you shall find it bring you cheer;
And I shall blush and droop my lashes lower
    And make responses, pleasing to your ear,
Knowing this simplest of all simple poses
Is always good for some three dozen roses.

What if I have made friends of love and laughter,
  That anciently have been such bitter foes,
And sent my merry verses flying after
  Your bated words like arrows after crows?
What if I have not met your sighs with sighing
  Nor once protested bliss too great to bear?
Comfort yourself with thinking I am lying
  And still make reticence my foremost care . . .
Comfort yourself in any way you choose;
  This love is greater treasure than you know.
A thing of patterns and dissolving views
  Clashing in fine kaleidoscopic show,
And those not lurid and not too confusing
Are definitely of the most amusing.

                              —Dorothy Kissling.

RENAISSANCE

Let's wrap love in a paper heart,
  And send it through the mail,
A red heart fringed with foamy lace,
  That shows a milky sail
With compass set for high romance,
  And moonbeams spattered over
A bush of roses or a field
  Dream-drenched with honeyed clover.

O let's be sweet and gay again,
  Pretending that it's smart
To live for love as ladies did
  When loving was an art;
When kisses meant a little more
  Than casual handshaking,
And candlelight and waltz time ruled
  When love was in the making.

Let's send love in an envelope
  The postman will deliver

At breakfast time, and let's restore
　The anatomic quiver.
Oh, let's send paper valentines
　On which a pink-edged cupid
Shoots darts at wistful maidens' hearts—
　Dear, let's be sweet and stupid!
　　　　　　　　　　—Helen Welshimer.

AN EXPLANATION

Her lips were so near
That . . . what else could I do?
You'll be angry, I fear,
But her lips were so near . . .
Well, I can't make it clear,
Or explain it to you,
But . . . her lips were so near
That . . . what else could I do?
　　　　　　　　　　—Walter Learned.

SUMMUM BONUM

All the breath and the bloom of the year in the
　　　　　bag of one bee:
All the wonder and wealth of the mine in the heart
　　　　　of one gem;
In the core of one pearl all the shade and the shine
　　　　　of the sea:
Breath and bloom, shade and shine, . . . wonder, wealth,
　and—how far above them . . .
　　Truth, that's brighter than gem
　　Trust, that's purer than pearl, . . .
Brightest truth, purest trust in the universe . . . all
　were for me
　　In the kiss of one girl.
　　　　　　　　　　—Robert Browning.

DREAMS AND A MOON

Dreams and a moon
  And you—
After all, these
  Will do!

They are all I need,
  Altho
There are other things
  I know,

Pleasant to have:
  The sea,
And the white bough
  Of a tree.

Books and
  A hearthfire bright
Are adjuncts
  Of delight,

But dreams and a moon
  And you
After all
  These will do!
           —Mary Carolyn Davies.

ON GOING TO CHURCH WITH IRENE

Our heads bow together,
  The lights are dim;
She's there (God protect her!)
  To worship Him.

But my soul is earthbound,
  I must aver;
I'm there (God forgive me!)
  To worship her.
           —William W. Wilcox.

PARADOX

When I'm with ordinary folk, my dear,
   I talk quite sensibly
Of mice and men and war and creeds
   And mental cruelty.

But when you come along, my dear,
   It's just the strangest thing
My tongue can't say the smallest words—
   But hear my proud heart sing!
                 —Sara Fair.

MEETING AT NIGHT

The grey sea and the long black land;
And the yellow half-moon large and low;
And the startled little waves that leap
In fiery ringlets from their sleep,
As I gain the cove with pushing prow,
And quench its speed i' the slushy sand.

Then a mile of warm sea-scented beach;
Three fields to cross till a farm appears;
A tap at the pane, the quick sharp scratch
And the blue spurt of a lighted match,
And a voice less loud, through its joys and fears,
Than the two hearts beating each to each!
                 —Robert Browning.

YOURS TRULY

Dear Sir: Received yours of the tenth
   And want to thank you for
The offer that you made us.
   We are anxious to hear more.

Please write us all the details
And we'll hasten to reply—
(Of course I love you, darling,
But the boss was passing by.)
—Evelyne Love Cooper.

ROMANCE

I will make you brooches and toys for your delight
Of bird-song at morning and star-shine at night.
I will make a palace fit for you and me,
Of green days in forests and blue days at sea.

I will make my kitchen, and you shall keep your room,
Where white flows the river and bright blows the broom,
And you shall wash your linen and keep your body white
In rainfall at morning and dewfall at night.

And this shall be for music when no one else is near,
The fine song for singing, the rare song to hear!
That only I remember, that only you admire,
Of the broad road that stretches and the roadside fire.
—Robert Louis Stevenson.

FOR YOU

"For you." Ah, little phrase that is
So big, I never hear
It on tongue, in air, or said
But that I know how dear

Are those two words, "for you," a kiss,
"For you" my love, for you:
Not all the big words that I know
Give those small ones their due—

This thing "for you," that thing. Ah give
    Me any other phrase
So vibrant with all timeless things,
    That speaks as tender praise.
                —George Elliston.

Shall I compare thee to a summer's day?
Thou art more lovely and more temperate:
Rough winds do shake the darling buds of May,
And summer's lease hath all too short a date:
Sometime too hot the eye of heaven shines,
And often is his gold complexion dimm'd;
And every fair from fair sometimes declines,
By chance, or nature's changing course untrimm'd;
But thy eternal summer shall not fade,
Nor lose possession of that fair thou ow'st,
Nor shall death brag thou wander'st in his shade,
When in eternal lines to time thou grow'st;
    So long as men can breathe, or eyes can see,
    So long lives this, and this gives life to thee.
                —William Shakespeare.

GENEROSITY

There isn't much that
I have learned,
And less that I have
Known . . .
But this I know; Love
Shares its joy,
And can't exist alone!
                —Peter A. Lea.

THERE CAME A DAY

And on that day were god-sired mountains born,
And baptised with a spray of meteor fire;

Grim chasms stretched and closed their maws, to trap
Dark thunders in a mad imprisonment,
And virgin rock was mangled in its pain
Of bringing canyons forth. Immeasurable
And fearful primal force! The clash of suns,
Unleased, announced that dim primordial dawn,
In ferment of volcanic genesis,
Of boiling seas and moulten moons and stars—
Within the maelstrom of immensity,
Where endings and beginnings have their birth—
You and winds, and flying clouds and I,
And embryonic dust all met that day.
                                        —Eva Riehle.

WHEN THERE IS MUSIC

Whenever there is music, it is you
    Who come between me and the sound of strings;
The cloudy portals part to let you through,
    Troubled and strange with long rememberings.
Your nearness gathers ghostwise down the room,
    And through the pleading violins they play,
There drifts the dim and delicate perfume
    That once was you, come dreamily astray.
Behind what thin and shadowy doors you wait
    That such frail things as these should set you free!
When all my need, like armies at a gate,
    Would storm in vain to bring you back to me;
When in this hush of strings you draw more near
Than any sound of music that I hear.
                                        —David Morton.

THIS IS MY LOVE FOR YOU

I have brought the wine
And the folded raiment fine,
Pilgrim staff and shoe—
This is my love for you.

I will smooth your bed,
Lay away your coverlid,
Sing the whole day through.
This is my love for you.

Mayhap in the night,
When the dark beats back the light,
I shall struggle too . . .
This is my love for you.

In your dream, once more,
Will a star lead to my door?
To stars and dreams be true.
This is my love for you.
                            —Grace Fallow Norton.

FATE

Two shall be born, the whole wide world apart,
And speak in different tongues and have no thought
Each of the other's being, and no heed.
And these, o'er unknown seas, to unknown lands
Shall cross, escaping wreck, defying death;
And all unconsciously shape every act
And bend each wandering step to this one end—
That, one day, out of darkness they shall meet
And read life's meaning in each other's eyes.

And two shall walk some narrow way of life
So nearly side by side, that should one turn
Ever so little space to left or right,
They needs must stand acknowledged, face to face.
And, yet, with wistful eyes that never meet
And groping hands that never clasp and lips
Calling in vain to ears that never hear,
They seek each other all their weary days
And die unsatisfied—and this is Fate!
                            —Susan M. Spalding.

ONE WAY

One way there was and that one way we went,
  One road there was and that one road we took
Where every tree with April weight was bent
  And new buds quivered as you gayly shook
White petals down—you called their shower rain,
  White rain, you said, to drench us through and
    through,
  With an eternal April, but I knew
That rain is but the tears of a great pain.

Today there are so many roads to take,
  Such narrow roads and each one without end,
And not an April bough that one might break
  For courage—how those branches used to bend!
What was it that once drenched us through and through,
And what were you to me and I to you?
                              —Gertrude Callaghan.

FATE

There was a time we might have met
  An hour we might have dined together;
Only it rained that night and I
  Stayed snug at home fearing the weather.

And once I saw you on the street
  Lilacs were out, the air was heady
I might have stopped to speak, but you
  Hailing a bus, were gone already.

I might have looked, you might have smiled,
  But we didn't and I can't see why
If we had known that you were you
  And I was I! Or did you pass and sigh?

It's odd to think we might have been
  Sun, Moon and Stars unto each other
Only I turned down one little street
  As you went up another.

—Unknown.

CHANCE

How many times we must have met
  Here on the street as strangers do,
Children of chance we were, who passed
  The door of heaven and never knew.

—Unknown.

DREAM

You will be gone
  Like the wind and its blowing;
Love cannot go with you
  Where you are going.

Love fits his step
  To the man in the street;
You ask the wings of the
  World for your feet.

Love is the width
  Of a house and a bed;
Why must the sky alone
  Cover your head?

Yet who can say
  Which is wisest or best,
The dream in the heart,
  Or the dream possessed?

—Dorothy Davis.

TO LUCASTA, ON GOING TO THE WARS

Tell me not, sweet, I am unkind,
    That from the nunnery
Of thy chaste breast and quiet mind
    To war and arms I fly.

True, a new mistress now I chase,
    The first foe in the field;
And with a stronger faith embrace
    A sword, a horse, a shield.

Yet this inconstancy is such
    As thou too shalt adore;
I could not love thee, dear, so much,
    Loved I not honor more.
                —Richard Lovelace.

FAR AND NEAR

What if the miles stretch out and bar
    That you and I should meet? Why, even still
You are beneath this very moon and star
    Which I am watching from my lonely hill,
    And I can say low with a happy thrill—
You are not far, dear heart, you are not far!
                —Thomas S. Jones, Jr.

—»»×««—

Out of my longing and my loneliness
    I make a song for you, and it shall be,
Frail as the touch of air, as the wind's caress,
    Mortal as music, timeless as the sea
That falters at your threshold. Out of dust,
    Out of the rich dark plenitude of earth
I fashion that which Autumn shall not rust
    Nor Winter doom implacably at birth.

Out of this waiting heart a dream shall rise
  And swiftly find its way to one still door
To look for recognition in your eyes;
  Out of my hope and out of the rich store
Of faith I send you this unshriven seed
That it may blossom in your hour of need.
                    —Sydney King Russell.

KISMET

Wherever you are, this song shall find you,
  Just as one day I shall stand
Close to your side to claim and bind you
  Lip upon lip and hand in hand'

Day after day I am drawing nearer
  Knowing that you are the only one
My heart can name as sweeter, dearer
  Than all things underneath the sun!

Whether a block or a world away
  True as I breathe and sure as fate,
I shall look in your eyes one day
  And find my world at your garden gate.

Whether a street or an earth apart
  A week, a year, whichever it be—
I know that I shall find the hand and heart
  Which God and Kismet meant for me!
                    —Unknown.

HEART'S WASHING

Shake out the old dreams, Heart, and hang them up;
  Out in the sane and comfortable sun,
They will blow dry of weeping. When the cup
  Of wonder spills no longer and the one

Who was not one, but everything, is mute,
  Emptied of vision, grave as those who die,
Call not your love back with some lonely flute—
  Shake out your dreams and hang them up to dry.

Sunlight is sure, and healing comes to make
  The heart a quiet place when dreams are dried,
So that one lives without the old heartbreak,
  Within the shell of love that all but died.
Sunlight is safe; but oh, beware, beware,
To hang out dreams if any moon be there!
                    —Helen Frazee-Bower.

SPECIALIST

    God, I've done everything that I could do
to keep our love from going on the rocks,
and tho I hate to have to bother You,
I cannot help myself. This fairly knocks
me off my feet, although I should have known
I was expecting too much. As a rule
I have more sense but I guess I have grown
so used to loving him that, like a fool,
I didn't stop to think it might not last.
I thought, "This time Love's really on the square
with me," but now I realize the vast
mistake I made, and so I send this prayer
in hopes it's not too late to ask Your aid.
If you'll just help me now, I'll not forget—
this seems to me, of all the times I've prayed
the most important thing I've asked, as yet.
So couldn't You, this once, see Your way clear
to save our love and make things as they were—
I've done my best and failed, that's why I'm here—
the miracles are Your department, Sir.
                    —Kathryn Kay.

CHERRY BARK

Do you remember the smell of cherry bark?
    I cannot describe it to you. I do not know
The words we murmured in the secret dark
    Some years ago.

I can only say that we were very tired,
    And the cherry bole was a pillow for your head,
And the noisy grass and its creatures were quiet . . .
        We desired
    No syllable said.

And the bitter-sweet smell of the cherry still edged the
        air,
    And the stars stood too tall to touch, and it seemed
        that we
Lay rooted and suckled in earth . . . and so we were
    Hushed as the tree . . .

Hushed for a moment . . . Where has that moment
        perished?
    We could not breathe . . . our hearts stopped . . .
        the planets were one . . .
In this whirling world where is the love we cherished?
    Where has quiet gone?
                            —Audrey Wurdemann.

HEARTBREAK

A heartbreak is a little thing,
    It only means that you
Will have no foolish songs to sing
    Or useless things to do.

A heartbreak means that you sit
    And watch a dream go by
And laugh because you know that it
    Will sicken soon, and die.

So small a thing a heartbreak is
    There is no word or touch,
No hand you clasp or smile you miss,
    Can move you very much.

A heartbreak means that where a kiss
    Has dealt you pain before
There is no thing—next world or this—
    Can hurt you any more.
               —Gertrude R. Ross.

PERHAPS

Perhaps we'll meet some day in some far year
    And hardly recognize each other's face;
Perhaps we'll grope a moment as we near,
    Endeavoring to recollect the place
Our ways once crossed. And then remembering
    We'll let our hands reach out and touch
As strangers might . . . so small, so brief a thing!
    One would not guess that it once meant so much.

I'll think, perhaps, "I'm so glad she went away!"
And you'll think, "He has aged!" and be glad too.
Then we shall find there's nothing much to say—
    much less to do.
So we shall part again—and neither guess
The other's sudden sense of loneliness.
               —Christie Lund Coles.

WHEN I AM DEAD, MY DEAREST

When I am dead, my dearest,
  Sing no sad songs for me;
Plant thou no roses at my head,
  Nor shady cypress-tree:
Be the green grass above me
  With showers and dewdrops wet:
And if thou wilt, remember,
  And if thou wilt, forget.

I shall not see the shadows,
  I shall not feel the rain;
I shall not hear the nightingale
  Sing on, as if in pain:
And dreaming through the twilight
  That doth not rise nor set,
Haply I may remember,
  And haply may forget.
                    —Christina Georgina Rossetti.

REMEMBER

Remember me when I am gone away,
  Gone far away into the silent land;
  When you can no more hold me by the hand,
Nor I half turn to go yet turning stay.
Remember me when no more day by day
  You tell me of our future that you planned:
  Only remember me; you understand
It will be late to counsel then or pray.
Yet if you should forget me for a while
  And afterwards remember, do not grieve:
  For if the darkness and corruption leave
  A vestige of the thoughts that once I had,
Better by far you should forget and smile
  Than that you should remember and be sad.
                    —Christina Georgina Rossetti.

I SHALL COME BACK

I shall come back, after the cool, dark loam,
　After the long, last pilgrimage with pain;
After the quiet sealing of the tomb,
　I shall come back to you in April rain.
And I shall throw myself against the glass
　Through which my vagrant heart can glimpse your
　　face,
But you will think it only winds that pass
　And rise to draw the shades beyond the lace.
I shall come back in birdsong, I shall come
　Suffused into the twilight's after-glow
Whispering above the grass though lips are dumb
　And you say, "She is dead," nor ever know
That I am close enough to feel your tear,
　And hear you whisper, "Were she only here!"
　　　　　　　　　　—Christie Lund Coles.

CONSTANCY

It is something sweet, when the world goes ill,
To know you are faithful and love me still;
To feel when the sunshine has left the skies
That the light is shining in your dear eyes;
Beautiful eyes, more dear to me,
Than all the wealth of the world could be.

It is something, dearest, to feel you near,
When life with its sorrow seems hard to bear;
To feel, when I falter, the clasp divine
Of your tender and trusting hand in mine;
Beautiful hand, more dear to me,
Than the tenderest thing on earth could be.

Sometimes, dearest, the world goes wrong,
For God gives grief with His gift of song.

And poverty, too, but your love is more
To me than riches and golden store;
Beautiful love, until death shall part,
It is mine—as you are—my own sweetheart.
                                        —Frank L. Stanton.

REMEMBERING

Stopped to hear a bird this morning
Trill his welcome to the dawning—
Thought perhaps he had a message
That would help me to forget.
But his song was all about you,
How I could not do without you
And the melody he chanted
Thrills my heart with longing yet.

Saw a flower with pearly edges.
Peeping out beneath the hedges—
Stopped to wonder at its beauty
So ethereal and so rare!
Almost I forgot my grieving
But I lower stooped in leaving,
And the fragrance of the blossom
Was the perfume of your hair.

Felt the morning breezes blowing,
Like a river gently flowing—
From the westward ever flowing,
To the ocean it would seek;
Stood with eager face up-lifted
To the sky where clouds were rifted
Then I knew the gentle zephyr
Was your touch upon my cheek.

Love of mine I can't forget you.
Had it chanced I had not met you

All my life would be a longing
For the thing I never knew.
Now I've known, there's no forgetting.
Through the pain there's no regretting
All my life will be a counting of the
Memories of you.

—Unknown.

CYNARA

Last night, ah, yesternight, betwixt her lips and mine
    There fell thy shadow, Cynara! thy breath was shed
Upon my soul between the kisses and the wine;
And I was desolate and sick of an old passion,
    Yea, I was desolate and bowed my head:
I have been faithful to thee, Cynara! in my fashion.

All night upon mine heart I felt her warm heart beat,
    Night-long within mine arms in love and sleep she lay;
Surely the kisses of her bought red mouth were sweet;
But I was desolate and sick of an old passion,
    When I awoke and found the dawn was gray:
I have been faithful to thee, Cynara! in my fashion.

I have forgot much, Cynara! gone with the wind,
    Flung roses, roses riotously with the throng,
Dancing, to put thy pale, lost lilies out of mind;
But I was desolate and sick of an old passion,
    Yea, all the time, because the dance was long:
I have been faithful to thee, Cynara! in my fashion.

I cried for madder music and for stronger wine,
    But when the feast is finished and the lamps expire,
Then falls thy shadow, Cynara! the night is thine;
And I am desolate and sick of an old passion,
    Yea, hungry for the lips of my desire:
I have been faithful to thee, Cynara! in my fashion.

—Ernest Dowson.

EVENING SONG

Look off, dear Love, across the sallow sands,
    And mark yon meeting of the sun and sea,
How long they kiss in sight of all the lands,
    Ah! longer, longer, we.

Now in the sea's red vintage melts the sun,
    As Egypt's pearl dissolved in rosy wine,
And Cleopatra night drinks all. 'Tis done,
    Love, lay thine hand in mine.

Come forth, sweet stars, and comfort heaven's heart;
    Glimmer, ye waves, round else unlighted sands.
O night! divorce our sun and sky apart,
    Never our lips, our hands.

—Sidney Lanier.

THE WOMAN YOU USED TO LOVE

Did you ever go back to the woman you used to
love, after it was all over—the heartache, the
self-conflict, the numbness, and all that—to
find in her a friend who understood, whose spirit
had grown sweeter, finer, truer than it used to be
in the old days when you loved but did not understand
how beautiful is such a friendship, and how rare?
There is a tenderness between you, and a sincerity
of truth, a subtle bond of union infinitely greater
in its strength and firmness than the old-time
passion ever bore. It isn't love as the world sees
it; it doesn't ruffle you or make you blind; there
is no swift and frequent alteration of ecstasy
and despair; no jealousy, or intoxication of the
senses, but just peace and natural sympathy, and
a subtle, quiet gladness of the soul. You never
quite forget her, even though you meet another

woman—which you always do—and marry her
for love. There is always the fragrant memory of
the other woman, whom you loved and lost, and
found again in a friend who understood.

—Unknown.

THE NIGHT HAS A THOUSAND EYES

The night has a thousand eyes,
  And the day but one;
Yet the light of the bright world dies
  With the dying sun.

The mind has a thousand eyes,
  And the heart but one;
Yet the light of a whole life dies
  When love is done.

—Francis William Bourdillon.

LOVE IS A LITTLE THING

"Love is a little thing," I heard it said,
  "A childish dream; a tremulous rainbow hung
In vanishing beauty; a confection fed
  To visionary women and the young.
But we are made for higher tasks; for those
  That clamor for an iron conquering;
Let weaklings sip the dew upon the rose;
  Life calls for heroes. Love's a little thing."

A little thing? Then naught at all are these:
Glory, with all her solemn flags unfurled,
God, and our dreams divine that toward Him roam,
The music of all the birds in all the trees;
The might of all the waters of the world
As one vast tidal wave deep-thundering home.

—Archibald Rutledge.

6. BOOTS AND SADDLES

Boots and Saddles

>»«<

WILLY AND THE LADY

Leave the lady, Willy, let the racket rip,
She is going to fool you, you have lost your grip,
Your brain is in a muddle and your heart is in a whirl,
Come along with me, Willy, never mind the girl!

  Come and have a Man-Talk,
  Come with those who can talk,
Light your pipe and listen, and the boys will see you
      through;
  Love is only chatter,
  Friends are all that matter,
Come and talk the Man-Talk, that's the cure for you!

Leave the lady, Willy, let her letter wait!
You'll forget your troubles when you get it straight,
The world is full of women, and the women full of wile;
Come along with me, Willy, we can make you smile!

  Come and have a Man-Talk,
  A rousing black-and-tan talk,
There are plenty there to teach you, there's a lot for you
      to do;
  Your head must stop its whirling
  Before you go-a-girling,
Come and talk the Man-Talk, that's the cure for you!

Come and have a Man-Talk
Forget your girl-divan talk,
You've got to get acquainted with another point of view!
Girls will only fool you,
We're the ones to school you,
Come and talk the Man-Talk, that's the cure for you!
—Gelett Burgess.

MID-WINTER

Let's build a jolly, crackling fire
With flames and shadows mounting higher;
We'll curl up in our cozy nook
With a fascinating book.

By the lamp's warm, rosy glow,
Oblivious of wind and snow,
We'll travel to the Orient
Or under Palms we'll pitch our tent.

No matter what the place or weather,
We'll be happy, if together;
We'll make our life's long, cherished span
One short, congenial caravan.
—Frances I. Shinn.

THE PEOPLE, YES

.   .   .   .

A Scotsman keeps the Sabbath and anything else he can
lay his hands on, say the English.
A fighting Frenchman runs away from even a she-goat,
say the Germans.
A Russian, say the Poles, can be cheated only by a gypsy,
a gypsy by a Jew, a Jew by a Greek, and a Greek by
the devil.
"If I owned Texas and hell I would rent Texas and move
to hell," said a famous general.

"That's right," wrote a Texas editor. "Every man for his
own country."

The Peloponnesians pulled these long ago, so did the
Russians, the Chinese, even the Fijis with rings in their
noses. Likewise:

An American is an Anglo-Saxon when an Englishman
wants something from him: or:

When a Frenchman has drunk too much he wants to
dance, a German to sing, a Spaniard to gamble, an
Italian to brag, an Irishman to fight, an American to
make a speech: or:

"What is dumber than a dumb Irishman?" "A smart
Swede."

These are in all tongues and regions of men. Often they
bring laughter and sometimes blood.

The propagandas of hate and war always monkey with
the buzz-saw of race and nationality, breed and kin,
seldom saying, "When in doubt hold your tongue."

In breathing spells of bloody combat between Christian
nations the order goes out: "Don't let the men in the
front-line trenches fraternize!"

The sea has fish for every man.
Every blade of grass has its share of dew.
The longest day must have its end.
Man's life? A candle in the wind, hoar-frost on stone.
Nothing more certain than death and nothing
more uncertain than the hour.
Men live like birds together in a wood; when
the time comes each takes his flight.
As wave follows wave, so new men take old men's places.

The copperfaces, the red men, handed us tobacco,
the weed for the pipe of friendship,
also the bah-tah-to, the potato, the spud.
Sunflowers came from Peruvians in ponchos.

Early Italians taught us of chestnuts,
walnuts and peaches being Persian mementoes,
Siberians finding for us what rye might do,
Hindus coming through with the cucumber,
Egyptians giving us the onion, the pea,
Arabians handing advice with one gift:
"Some like it, some say it's just spinach."
    To the Chinese we have given
    kerosene, bullets, bibles
    and they have given us radishes, soy beans, silk,
    poems, paintings, proverbs, porcelain, egg foo yong,
    gunpowder, Fourth of July firecrackers, fireworks,
    and labor gangs for the first Pacific railways.
    Now we may thank these people
    or reserve our thanks
    and speak of them as outsiders
    and imply the request,
"Would you just as soon get off the earth?"
holding ourselves aloof in pride of distinction
saying to ourselves this costs us nothing
as though hate has no cost
as though hate ever grew anything worth growing.
Yes we may say this trash is beneath our notice
or we may hold them in respect and affection
as fellow creepers on a commodious planet
saying, "Yes, you too are people."

    "When God finished making the world
    He had a few stinking scraps of mud left over
    and used it to make a yellow dog"
        (and when they hate any race or nation
        they name that race or nation
        in place of the yellow dog).
They say and they say and the juice of prejudice drips
    from it.
They say and they say and in the strut of fool pride spit
    in the wind.

And the first of the seven rottening sins is this one: pride.
They set up a razzle-dazzle and get caught in their own
  revolving mirrors.
"We are the greatest city, the greatest people. Nothing
  like us ever was."
They set out for empire not knowing men and nations
  can die of empire.
And the earth is strewn with the burst bladders of the
  puffed-up.

> The best preacher is the heart,
> say the Jews of faith.
> The best teacher is time.
> The best book is the world.
> The best friend is God.

> The three worst waters,
> say the Irish:
> brown rain at the fall of the leaf,
> black rain at the springing of roots,
> the grey rain of May.

Love, a cough, an itch, or a fat paunch cannot be hid.
Love, a cough, smoke, money or poverty, are hard to hide.

Three things you can't nurse: an old woman, a hen, and
  a sheep.
Three who have their own way: a mule, a pig, and a miser.
Three to stay way from: a snake, a man with an oily
  tongue, and a loose woman.
Three things always pleasing: a cat's kittens, a goat's kid,
  and a young woman.
The three prettiest dead: a little child, a salmon, a
  black cock.
Three of the coldest things: a man's knee, a cow's horn,
  and a dog's nose.
Three who come unbidden: love, jealousy, fear.

Three soon passing away: the beauty of a woman, the rainbow, the echo of the woods.
Three worth wishing: knowledge, grain, and friendship.

Men are made of clay but women are made of men.
An old friend is better than two new ones.
He gets up early who pleases everybody.

Two fools in a house are a couple too many.
"I have forgotten your name" is better than "I don't remember you."
Some can eat nails, others break their teeth on applesauce.
"Run home, your house is on fire." "No, that can't be. I locked the house when I left home."
"So now he's dead." "Yes." "What did he die of?" "The want of breath."
There are two good men, say the Chinese, one dead, the other not born yet.
The seller can get along with one eye, the buyer needs a hundred.
The ragged colt may prove a good horse.
The hasty bitch brings forth blind whelps.

He's eaten off many a dish and never washed a dish.
He's the sort that would haul rock with a race-horse.
It would be like him to drown in a spoonful of water.
If he had learned the hatter's trade, men would have been born without heads.
Ugly? Sleep stays away from him till he covers his face.
Poor? He can't raise money enough to buy lumber for a backhouse.
Big feet? Buying shoes he don't ask for a number, he says, "Lemme see the biggest you got."

"Slave, I have bought you."
"God knows you have."

"Now you belong to me."
"God knows I do."
"And you'll not run away?"
"God knows."

In the days of the far off Pharaohs
in the days of Nebuchadnezzar
the king who ate grass
and reconsidered many former decisions—
one of the masters straddling a slave:
  "I think about you often
  and I would be willing
  to do many kind things
  almost anything for you."
    And the man under:
"Almost anything except get off my back."
                —Carl Sandburg.

MR. FLOOD'S PARTY

Old Eben Flood, climbing alone one night
  Over the hill between the town below
And the forsaken upland hermitage
  That held as much as he should ever know
On earth again of home, paused warily.
  The road was his with not a native near;
And Eben, having leisure, said aloud,
  For no man else in Tilbury Town to hear:

"Well, Mr. Flood, we have the harvest moon
  Again, and we may not have many more;
The bird is on the wing, the poet says,
  And you and I have said it here before.
Drink to the bird." He raised up to the light
  The jug that he had gone so far to fill,
And answered huskily: "Well, Mr. Flood,
  Since you propose it, I believe I will."

Alone, as if enduring to the end
   A valiant armor of scarred hopes outworn,
He stood there in the middle of the road
   Like Roland's ghost winding a silent horn.
Below him, in the town among the trees,
   Where friends of other days had honored him,
A phantom salutation of the dead
   Rang thinly till old Eben's eyes were dim.

Then, as a mother lays her sleeping child
   Down tenderly, fearing it may awake,
He set the jug down slowly at his feet
   With trembling care, knowing that most things break;
And only when assured that on firm earth
   It stood, as the uncertain lives of men
Assuredly did not, he paced away,
   And with his hand extended paused again:

"Well, Mr. Flood, we have not met like this
   In a long time; and many a change has come
To both of us, I fear, since last it was
   We had a drop together. Welcome home!"
Convivially returning with himself,
   Again he raised the jug up to the light;
And with an acquiescent quaver said:
   "Well, Mr. Flood, if you insist, I might.

"Only a very little, Mr. Flood—
   For auld lang syne. No more, sir; that will do."
So, for the time, apparently it did,
   And Eben evidently thought so too;
For soon amid the silver loneliness
   Of night he lifted up his voice and sang,
Secure, with only two moons listening,
   Until the whole harmonious landscape rang—

"For auld lang syne." The weary throat gave out,
  The last word wavered, and the song was done.

He raised again the jug regretfully
  And shook his head, and was again alone.
There was not much that was ahead of him,
  And there was nothing in the town below—
Where strangers would have shut the many doors
  That many friends had opened long ago.
                    —Edwin Arlington Robinson.

MOONSHINER

They found him close against the mountain-side,
Unkempt and raw-boned in his frayed blue jeans,
Idling beside a rudely fashioned still
With rusty cauldron and corroding pipes.
"It's none of mine," he pointed to the mash,
"I come up here a-lookin' fer some shoats."

"Aw, come, don't pull that worn-out stuff!" they jeered,
And led him down the rugged, leaf-strewn path
To where his scrawny wife was washing clothes
Behind a two-room shanty. At her feet
A grimy girl was playing with a cat,
While from within a baby's feeble cries
Came fitfully. Two boys in overalls
Were cutting wood, but paused with bulging eyes
To see their father and the sheriff's men.
"We caught him at the still. He'll have to go."

He lay behind the bars for seven weeks
Before his case was called. His hapless brood,
Like pallid shades from Limbo, came to court;
The thin-clad mother with her snuff-stained lips,
The baby worrying her withered breast;
The listless child; the hollow-chested boys—

While their provider shrank into his chair,
Drawing a shabby coat about his neck.

When all the evidence was in and guilt
Was proved beyond the faintest shade of doubt,
The jury filed into a guarded room.
The haggard mother sniffed against her hand;
The baby cried, the small girl squirmed and whined,
The ragged boys sat stolid, open-mouthed,
The jurymen filed back into the room.
Unflinchingly the foreman rose and said:
"We, the Jury, find the defendant not guilty."
                    —Louise Crenshaw Ray.

THE CREMATION OF SAM McGEE

There are strange things done in the midnight sun
    By the men who toil for gold;
The Arctic trails have their secret tales
    That would make your blood run cold;

The Northern Lights have seen queer sights,
    But the queerest they ever did see
Was the night on the marge of Lake Lebarge
    I cremated Sam McGee.

Now Sam McGee was from Tennessee, where the cotton
    blooms and blows,
Why he left his home in the South to roam 'round the
    Pole, God only knows.
He was always cold, but the land of gold seemed to hold
    him like a spell;
Though he'd often say in his homely way that "he'd
    sooner live in hell."

On Christmas Day we were mushing our way over the
    Dawson Trail.

Talk of your cold! through the parka's fold it stabbed like
a driven nail.
If our eyes we'd close, then the lashes froze till sometimes
we couldn't see;
It wasn't much fun, but the only one to whimper was
Sam McGee.

And that very night, as we lay packed tight in our robes
beneath the snow,
And the dogs were fed, and the stars o'erhead were
dancing heel and toe,
He turned to me, and "Cap," says he, "I'll cash in this
trip, I guess;
And if I do, I'm asking that you won't refuse my last
request."

Well, he seemed so low that I couldn't say no; then he
says with a sort of moan:
"It's the cursed cold, and it's got right hold till I'm
chilled clean through to the bone.
Yet 'tain't being dead—it's my awful dread of the icy
grave that pains;
So I want you to swear that, foul or fair, you'll cremate
my last remains."

A pal's last need is a thing to heed, so I swore I would not
fail;
And we started on at the streak of dawn; but God! he
looked ghastly pale.
He crouched on the sleigh, and he raved all day of his
home in Tennessee;
And before nightfall a corpse was all that was left of
Sam McGee.

There wasn't a breath in that land of death, and I hurried, horror-driven,

With a corpse half hid that I couldn't get rid, because of
a promise I'd given;
It was lashed to the sleigh, and it seemed to say: "You
may tax your brawn and brains,
But you promised true, and it's up to you to cremate
those last remains."

Now a promise made is a debt unpaid, and the trail has
it own stern code.
In the days to come, though my lips were dumb, in my
heart how I cursed that load.
In the long, long night, by the lone firelight, while the
huskies round in a ring,
Howled out their woes to the homeless snows—O God!
how I loathed the thing.

And every day that quiet clay seemed heavier and
heavier to grow;
And on I went, though the dogs were spent and the grub
was getting low;
The trail was bad, and I felt half mad, but I swore I
would not give in;
And I'd often sing to the hateful thing, and it hearkened
with a grin.

Till I came to the marge of Lake Lebarge, and a derelict
there lay;
It was jammed in the ice, but I saw in a trice it was called
the "Alice May."
And I looked at it, and I thought a bit, and I looked at
my frozen chum;
Then "Here," said I, with a sudden cry, "is my cre-
ma-tor-e-um."

Some planks I tore from the cabin floor, and I lit the
boiler fire;

Some coal I found that was lying around, and I heaped
  the fuel higher;
The flames just soared, and the furnace roared—such a
  blaze you seldom see;
And I burrowed a hole in the glowing coal, and I stuffed
  in Sam McGee.

Then I made a hike, for I didn't like to hear him sizzle so;
And the heavens scowled, and the huskies howled, and
  the wind began to blow.
It was icy cold, but the hot sweat rolled down my cheeks,
  and I don't know why;
And the greasy smoke in an inky cloak went streaking
  down the sky.

I do not know how long in the snow I wrestled with
  grisly fear;
But the stars came out and they danced about ere again
  I ventured near;
I was sick with dread, but I bravely said: "I'll just take
  a peep inside.
I guess he's cooked, and it's time I looked," . . . then
  the door I opened wide.

And there sat Sam, looking cold and calm, in the heart
  of the furnace roar;
And he wore a smile you could see a mile, and he said:
  "Please close that door!
It's fine in here, but I greatly fear you'll let in the cold
  and storm—
Since I left Plumtree down in Tennessee, it's the first
  time I've been warm."

  There are strange things done in the midnight sun
    By the men who toil for gold;
  The Arctic trails have their secret tales
    That would make your blood run cold;

The Northern Lights have seen queer sights,
  But the queerest they ever did see
Was that night on the marge of Lake Lebarge
  I cremated Sam McGee.
                          —Robert W. Service.

CASEY AT THE BAT

It looked extremely rocky for the Mudville nine that day;
The score stood two to four, with but an inning left to
  play.
So, when Cooney died at second, and Burrows did the
  same,
A pallor wreathed the features of the patrons of the game.

A straggling few got up to go, leaving there the rest,
With that hope which springs eternal within the human
  breast.
For they thought: "If only Casey could get a whack at
  that,"
They'd put up even money now, with Casey at the bat.

But Flynn preceded Casey, and likewise so did Blake,
And the former was a pudd'n, and the latter was a fake.
So on that stricken multitude a deathlike silence sat;
For there seemed but little chance of Casey's getting to
  the bat.

But Flynn let drive a "single," to the wonderment of all.
And the much-despised Blakey "tore the cover off the
  ball."
And when the dust had lifted, and they saw what had
  occurred,
There was Blakey safe at second, and Flynn a-huggin'
  third.

Then from the gladdened multitude went up a joyous
  yell—

It rumbled in the mountaintops, it rattled in the dell;
It struck upon the hillside and rebounded on the flat;
For Casey, mighty Casey, was advancing to the bat.

There was ease in Casey's manner as he stepped into his
place,
There was pride in Casey's bearing and a smile on Casey's
face;
And when responding to the cheers he lightly doffed his
hat,
No stranger in the crowd could doubt 'twas Casey at
the bat.

Ten thousand eyes were on him as he rubbed his hands
with dirt,
Five thousand tongues applauded when he wiped them
on his shirt;
Then when the writhing pitcher ground the ball into his
hip,
Defiance glanced in Casey's eye, a sneer curled Casey's
lip.

And now the leather-covered sphere came hurtling
through the air,
And Casey stood a-watching it in haughty grandeur
there.
Close by the sturdy batsman the ball unheeded sped;
"That ain't my style," said Casey. "Strike one," the
umpire said.

From the benches, black with people, there went up a
muffled roar,
Like the beating of the storm waves on the stern and
distant shore.
"Kill him! kill the umpire!" shouted someone on the
stand;

And it's likely they'd have killed him had not Casey
raised his hand.

With a smile of Christian charity great Casey's visage
shone;
He stilled the rising tumult, he made the game go on;
He signaled to the pitcher, and once more the spheroid
flew;
But Casey still ignored it, and the umpire said, "Strike
two."

"Fraud!" cried the maddened thousands, and the echo
answered "Fraud!"
But one scornful look from Casey and the audience was
awed;
They saw his face grow stern and cold, they saw his
muscles strain,
And they knew that Casey wouldn't let the ball go by
again.

The sneer is gone from Casey's lips, his teeth are clenched
in hate,
He pounds with cruel vengeance his bat upon the plate;
And now the pitcher holds the ball, and now he lets it go,
And now the air is shattered by the force of Casey's blow.

Oh, somewhere in this favored land the sun is shining
bright,
The band is playing somewhere, and somewhere hearts
are light;
And somewhere men are laughing, and somewhere
children shout,
But there is no joy in Mudville: mighty Casey has struck
out.

                                    —Ernest Lawrence Thayer.

GUNGA DIN

You may talk o' gin and beer
When you're quartered safe out 'ere,
An' you're sent to penny-fights an' Aldershot it;
But when it comes to slaughter
You will do your work on water,
An' you'll lick the bloomin' boots of 'im that's got it.
Now in Injia's sunny clime,
Where I used to spend my time
A-servin' of 'Er Majesty the Queen,
Of all them black-faced crew
The finest man I knew
Was our regimental bhisti, Gunga Din.
  He was "Din! Din! Din!
 "You limpin' lump o' brick-dust, Gunga Din!
  "Hi! Slippy hitherao!
  "Water, get it! Panee lao
 "You squidgy-nosed old idol, Gunga Din."

The uniform 'e wore
Was nothin' much before,
An' rather less than 'arf o' that be'ind,
For a piece o' twisty rag
An' a goatskin water-bag
Was all the field-equipment 'e could find.
When the sweatin' troop-train lay
In a sidin' through the day,
Where the 'eat would make your bloomin' eyebrows
 crawl,
We shouted "Harry By!"
Till our throats were bricky-dry,
Then we wopped 'im 'cause 'e couldn't serve us all.
  It was "Din! Din! Din!
 "You 'eathen, where the mischief 'ave you been?
  "You put some juldee in it

"Or I'll marrow you this minute
"If you don't fill up my helmet, Gunga Din!"

'E would dot an' carry one
Till the longest day was done,
An' 'e didn't seem to know the use o' fear.
If we charged or broke or cut,
You could bet your bloomin' nut,
'E'd be waitin' fifty paces right flank rear
With 'is mussick on 'is back,
'E would skip with our attack,
An' watch us till the bugles made "Retire"
An' for all 'is dirty 'ide
'E was white, clear white, inside
When 'e went to tend the wounded under fire!
    It was "Din! Din! Din!"
  With the bullets kickin' dust-spots on the green
    When the cartridges ran out,
    You could hear the front-ranks shout,
  "Hi! ammunition-mules an' Gunga Din!"

I sha'n't forgit the night
When I dropped be'ind the fight
With a bullet where my belt-plate should 'a' been.
I was chokin' mad with thirst,
An' the man that spied me first
Was our good old grinnin', gruntin' Gunga Din.
'E lifted up my 'ead,
An' he plugged me where I bled,
An' 'e guv me 'arf-a-pint o' water green.
It was crawlin' and it stunk,
But of all the drinks I've drunk,
I'm gratefullest to one from Gunga Din.
    It was "Din! Din! Din!"
  "'Ere's a beggar with a bullet through 'is spleen;
    "'E's chawin' up the ground,

"An' 'e's kickin' all around:
"For Gawd's sake git the water, Gunga Din!"

'E carried me away
To where a dooli lay,
An' a bullet come an' drilled the beggar clean.
'E put me safe inside,
An' just before 'e died,
"I 'ope you liked your drink," sez Gunga Din.
So I'll meet 'im later on
At the place where 'e is gone—
Where it's always double drill and no canteen.
'E'll be squattin' on the coals
Givin' drink to poor damned souls,
An' I'll get a swig in hell from Gunga Din!
    Yes, Din! Din! Din!
You Lazarushian-leather Gunga Din!
    Though I've belted you and flayed you,
    By the livin' Gawd that made you,
You're a better man than I am, Gunga Din!
                                —Rudyard Kipling.

NOAH AN' JONAH AN' CAP'N JOHN SMITH

Noah an' Jonah an' Cap'n John Smith
Mariners, travelers, magazine of myth,
Settin' up in Heaven, chewin' and a-chawin'
Eatin' their terbaccy, talkin' and a-jawin';
Settin' by a crick, spittin' in the worter,
Talkin' tall an' tactless, as saints hadn't orter,
Lollin' in the shade, baitin' hooks and anglin',
Occasionally friendly, occasionally wranglin'.

Noah took his halo from his old bald head
An' swatted of a hoppergrass an' knocked it dead,
An' he baited of his hook, and he spoke an' said:

"When I was the Skipper of the tight leetle Ark
I useter fish for papus, useter fish fer shark,
Often I have ketched in a single hour on Monday
Sharks enough to feed the fambly till Sunday—
To feed all the sarpints, the giers an' donkeys,
To feed all the zebras, the insects an' monkeys,
To feed all the varmints, bears an' gorillars,
To feed all the camels, cats an' amadillers,
To give all the pelicans stews for their gizzards,
To feed all the owls an' catamounts an' lizards,
To feed all the humans, their babies an' their nusses,
To feed all the houn' dawgs an' hippopotamusses,
To feed all the oxens, feed all the asses,
Feed all the bison an' leetle hoppergrasses—
Always I ketched, in half a hour on Monday
All that the fambly could gormandize till Sunday!"

Jonah took his harp, to strum and to string her,
An' Cap'n John Smith teched his nose with his finger,
Cap'n John Smith, he hommed some an' hawed some,
An' he bit off a chaw, an' he chewed some and chawed
     some:—
"When I was to China, when I was to Guinea,
When I was to Java, an' also in Verginney,
I teached all the natives how to be ambitious,
I learned 'em my trick of ketchin' devilfishes.
I've fitten tigers, I've fitten bears,
I have fitten sarpints an' wolves in their lairs,
I have fit with wild men an' hippopotamusses,
But the perilousest varmints is the bloody octopusses!
I'd rub my forehead with phosphorescent light
An' plunge into the ocean an' seek 'em out at night!
I ketched 'em in grottoes, I ketched 'em in caves,
I used fer to strangle 'em underneath the waves!
When they seen the bright light blazin' on my forehead
They used ter to rush at me, screamin' something horrid!

Tentacles wavin', teeth white an' gnashin',
Hollerin' an' bellerin', wallerin' an' splashin'!
I useter grab 'em as they rushed from their grots,
Ketch all their legs an' tie 'em into knots!"

Noah looked at Jonah, an' said not a word,
But if winks made noises, a wink had been heard.
Jonah took the hook from a mudcat's middle
An' strummed on the strings of his hallelujah fiddle;
Jonah give his whiskers a backhand wipe
An' cut some plug terbaccer an' crammed it in his pipe!
—(Noah an' Jonah an' Cap'n John Smith,
Fisherman an' travelers, narreratin' myth,
Settin' up in Heaven all eternity,
Fishin' in the shade, contented as could be!
Spittin' their terbaccer in the little shaded creek,
Stoppin' of their yarns fer ter hear the ripples speak!
I hope for Heaven, when I think of this—
You folks bound hellward, a lot of fun you'll miss!)

Jonah, he decapitates that mudcat's head,
An' gets his pipe ter drawin'; an' this is what he said:
"Excuse me ef your stories don't excite me much!
Excuse me ef I seldom agitate fer such!
You think yer fishermen! . . . I won't argue none!
I won't even tell yer the half o' what I done!
You has careers dangerous an' checkered!
All as I will say is: Go and read my record!
You think yer fishermen! You think yer great!
All I asks is this: Has one of ye been bait?
Cap'n Noah, Cap'n John, I heered when ye hollored;
What I asks is this: Has one of ye been swallered?
It's mighty purty fishin' with little hooks an' reels.
It's mighty easy fishin' with little rods an' creels.

It's mighty pleasant ketchin' mudcats fer yer dinners.
But this here is my challenge fer saints an' fer sinners,
Which one of ye has v'yaged in a varmint's inners?
When I seen a big fish, tough as Methooslum,
I used fer to dive into his oozly-goozlum!
When I seen the strong fish, wallopin' like a lummicks,
I useter foller 'em, dive into their stummicks!
I could v'yage an' steer 'em, I could understand 'em,
I useter navigate 'em, I useter land 'em!
Don't you pester me with any more narration!
Go git famous! Git a reputation!"

Cap'n John he grinned his hat brim beneath,
Clicked his tongue of silver on his golden teeth;
Noah an' Jonah an' Cap'n John Smith,
Strummin' golden harps, narreratin' myth!
Settin' by the shallows forever an' forever,
Swappin' yarns an' fishin' in a little river!
                                    —Don Marquis.

MY LAST DUCHESS

FERRARA

That's my last Duchess painted on the wall,
Looking as if she were alive. I call
That piece a wonder, now: Fra Pandolf's hands
Worked busily a day, and there she stands.
Will 't please you sit and look at her? I said
"Fra Pandolf" by design, for never read
Strangers like you that pictured countenance,
The depth and passion of its earnest glance,
But to myself they turned (since none puts by
The curtain I have drawn for you, but I)
And seemed as they would ask me, if they durst,
How such a glance came there; so, not the first
Are you to turn and ask thus. Sir, 'twas not

Her husband's presence only, called that spot
Of joy into the Duchess' cheek: perhaps
Fra Pandolf chanced to say "Her mantle laps
Over my lady's wrist too much," or "Paint
must never hope to reproduce the faint
Half-flush that dies along her throat:" such stuff
Was courtesy, she thought, and cause enough
For calling up that spot of joy. She had
A heart—how shall I say?—too soon made glad,
Too easily impressed; she liked whate'er
She looked on, and her looks went everywhere.
Sir, 'twas all one! My favour at her breast,
The dropping of the daylight in the west,
The bough of cherries some officious fool
Broke in the orchard for her, the white mule
She rode with round the terrace—all and each
Would draw from her alike the approving speech,
Or blush, at least. She thanked men,—good! but thanked
Somehow—I know not how—as if she ranked
My gift of a nine-hundred-years-old name
With anybody's gift. Who'd stoop to blame
This sort of trifling? Even had you skill
In speech—(which I have not)—to make your will
Quite clear to such an one, and say. "Just this
or that in you disgusts me; here you miss,
Or there exceed the mark"—and if she let
Herself be lessoned so, nor plainly set
Her wits to yours, forsooth, and made excuse,
—E'en then would be some stooping; and I choose
Never to stoop. Oh sir, she smiled, no doubt,
Whene'er I passed her; but who passed without
Much the same smile? This grew; I gave commands;
Then all smiles stopped together. There she stands
As if alive. Will 't please you rise? We'll meet
The company below, then. I repeat,
The Count your master's known munificence

Is ample warrant that no just pretence
Of mine for dowry will be disallowed;
Though his fair daughter's self, as I avowed
At starting, is my object. Nay, we'll go
Together down, sir. Notice Neptune, though,
Taming a sea-horse, thought a rarity
Which Claus of Innsbruck cast in bronze for me!

—Robert Browning.

TWIXT MAN AND MAN

I

My dear Mrs. Kenneth: This goes to you tonight with a box of arbutus blossoms—the flowers you told me you loved best. As your flowers, I thought of them while I searched the woods for them. You will not refuse them a welcome. Let them tell you if they can—if anything can—of my reverence for you. Their fragrance is but faintly typical of the sweetness your life has breathed upon mine. In the presence of these pure blossoms—in your presence I tremble as I allude to the last dance on the lawn.

Perhaps you will forgive me for the exquisite joy of that half-hour in the moonlight, when I tell you that since yesterday, when I learned the truth, my hair is almost white. You were so young; you had come all the way from Washington, I did not catch your name, and then when you were chosen maid of honor, I felt sure. I am a wordly fellow, Mrs. Kenneth, but I think as I sit writing here alone tonight, that in that other world where souls are unveiled, you will not blush to have inspired the worship of even a worldly fellow's heart— the worship my heart will always give you.

Faithfully yours,
John Thurston

March 8, 1902
Calumet Club, New York

II

My dear Mr. Thurston: Your box of arbutus came last Sunday morning. Dolly, my wife, died the night before. When I read your letter, I laid the blossoms in her hands. I, too, am a worldly man. I had grown used, I fear, to the precious things in life. I cannot put a finger on my regrets—I never knowingly hurt her, but as your letter lies before me now, it comes to me with bitter pain that I did not always worship on my knees.

In that world where souls are unveiled, Dolly sees clearly now, and it may be that she knows you loved her best. God forgive me! She was worth the homage of both our lives. Her death leaves me quite alone. When you are in Washington you can find me at the University Club.

Yours truly,

Richard Kenneth

March 12, 1902

—Unknown.

ODE

We are the music-makers,
  And we are the dreamers of dreams,
Wandering by lone sea-breakers,
  And sitting by desolate streams;

World-losers and world-forsakers,
  On whom the pale moon gleams;
Yet we are the movers and shakers
  Of the world for ever, it seems.

With wonderful deathless ditties
We build up the world's great cities,
  And out of a fabulous story
  We fashion an empire's glory:

One man with a dream, at pleasure,
   Shall go forth and conquer a crown
And three with a new song's measure
   Can trample an empire down.

We, in the ages lying
   In the buried past of the earth,
Built Nineveh with our sighing,
   And Babel itself with our mirth;
And o'erthrew them with prophesying
   To the old of the new world's worth;
For each age is a dream that is dying,
   Or one that is coming to birth.
             —Arthur O'Shaughnessy.

THE BEST ROAD OF ALL

I like a road that leads away to prospects white and fair,
A road that is an ordered road, like a nun's evening
   prayer;
But best of all I love a road that leads to God knows
   where.

You come upon it suddenly—you cannot seek it out;
It's like a secret still unheard and never noised about;
But when you see it, gone at once is every lurking doubt.

It winds beside some rushing stream where aspens lightly
   quiver;
It follows many a broken field by many a shining river;
It seems to lead you on and on, forever and forever.

You tramp along its dusty way beneath the shadowy
   trees,
And hear beside you chattering birds or happy booming
   bees,
And all around you golden sounds, the green leaves'
   litanies.

And here's a hedge and there's a cot; and then, strange,
     sudden turns—
A dip, a rise, a little glimpse where the red sunset burns;
A bit of sky at evening time, the scent of hidden ferns.

A winding road, a loitering road, the finger mark of God,
Traced when the Maker of the world leaned over ways
     untrod.
See! Here He smiled His glowing smile, and lo, the
     golden-rod!

I like a road that wanders straight; the king's highway is
     fair,
And lovely are the sheltered lanes that take you here and
     there;
But best of all I love a road that leads to God knows
     where.

                              —Charles Hanson Towne.

GYPSY LAMENT

I knew a gypsy lad last spring,
     With laughter in his eyes,
He made a rope of silver stars,
     And climbed to reach the skies.
He made a road of tangled silk,
     Burned-gold at dawn, and then,
He said: "There are lands that I must see
     But I'll be back again!

"There's gold within the Persian moon,
     Dreams older than Cathay,
Rendezvous with Hindu maids—
     I think I'll start today.
There are trysts with girls I've kissed
     In Cairo and Peru,
Pledges to a sorceress
     Before I dreamed of you!"

He had roving ways and songs,
  And he rode at dawn.
When the moon turned white again
  The gypsy lad was gone.
He rode away a troubadour
  Who hummed a foolish song . . .
My heart's not the only one
  That he took along!
            —Helen Welshimer.

OUT WHERE THE WEST BEGINS

Out where the handclasp's a little stronger,
Out where the smile dwells a little longer,
  That's where the West begins;
Out where the sun is a little brighter,
Where the snows that fall are a trifle whiter,
Where the bonds of home are a wee bit tighter,
  That's where the West begins.

Out where the skies are a trifle bluer,
Out where friendship's a little truer,
  That's where the West begins;
Out where a fresher breeze is blowing,
Where there's laughter in every streamlet flowing,
Where there's more of reaping and less of sowing,
  That's where the West begins.

Out where the world is in the making,
Where fewer hearts in despair are aching,
  That's where the West begins;
Where there's more of singing and less of sighing,
Where there's more of giving and less of buying,
And a man makes friends without half trying—
  That's where the West begins.
            —Arthur Chapman.

WANDERLUST

Beyond the East the sunrise, beyond the West the sea,
And East and West the wanderlust that will not let
me be;
It works in me like madness, dear, to bid me say
good-bye!
For the seas call and the stars call, and oh, the call of
the sky!

I know not where the white road runs, nor what the blue
hills are,
But man can have the sun for friend, and for his guide a
star;
And there's no end of voyaging when once the voice is
heard,
For the river calls and the road calls, and oh, the call
of a bird!

Yonder the long horizon lies, and there by night and day
The old ships draw me home again, and the young ships
sail away;
And come I may, but go I must, and if men ask you why,
You may put the blame on the stars and the sun and the
white road and the sky!

—Gerald Gould.

NIGHT JOURNEY

I do not know why we went, nor why
We went at night, but the midnight sky
I shall remember till I die.

The mottled moon and the light clouds fleet,
The white fog rolled like a winding-sheet,
And the red road silver before our feet.

The croon of the crickets in dry, dead grass,
The note of a night-bird as we passed,
I shall remember to the last.

I do not know why we went, nor why
We went at night, but your heart's hushed cry
My heart heard, and made reply.
                    —Ellen Francis Gilbert.

THE FLAG

The wings of the ships that sail the sky
  And the vessels that cruise the seas,
The tramp of feet where long armies come,
  And the wind in the singing trees,
The odor that comes from soil, new-turned,
  The hum of machinery's wheel,
A soldier's blood and a woman's faith,
  Courage and dreams and steel . . . .

Out of their warp the flag is made,
  Out of their web there comes
The banner that floats when brave men march
  To the tune of the martial drums.
May we have strength to keep it high,
  God, let no dull threads mar
The flag of a thousand victories,
  Keep it a guiding star.
                    —Helen Welshimer.

RELIEVING GUARD

Came the Relief. "What, Sentry, ho!
  How passed the night through the long waking?"
"Cold, cheerless, dark—as may befit
  The hour before the dawn is breaking."

"No sight? no sound?" "No; nothing save
  The plover from the marshes calling,
And in yon western sky, about
  An hour ago, a star was falling."

"A star? There's nothing strange in that."
  "No, nothing; but, above the thicket,
Somehow it seemed to me that God
  Somewhere had just relieved a picket."
                        —Francis Bret Harte.

WISH

Sunlight about you, wherever you are,
And the tree-like peace of the morning star,
Ever within you the song of the thrush—
And sweet rest, friend, when the day sounds hush.

Green roads before you, wherever you walk,
And an old friend near when the heart must talk,
Love's coin be your wealth constantly—
And sunlight about you, wherever you be!
                        —Bert Cooksley.

VAGABOND'S HOUSE

When I have a house . . . as I sometime may . . .
I'll suit my fancy in every way.
I'll fill it with things that have caught my eye
In drifting from Iceland to Molokai.
It won't be correct or in period style
But . . . oh, I've thought for a long, long while
Of all the corners and all the nooks,
Of all the bookshelves and all the books,
The great big table, the deep soft chairs
And the Chinese rug at the foot of the stairs,
(it's an old, old rug from far Chow Wan
that a Chinese princess once walked on.)

     .   .   .   .

I'll want a wood-box, scarred and rough,
For leaves and bark and odorous stuff
Like resinous knots and cones and gums
To chuck on the flames when winter comes.
And I hope a cricket will stay around
For I love its creaky lonesome sound.

There'll be driftwood powder to burn on logs
And a shaggy rug for a couple of dogs,
Boreas, winner of prize and cup,
And Micky, a loveable gutter-pup.
Thoroughbreds, both of them right from the start,
One by breeding, the other by heart.

.   .   .   .

There are times when only a dog will do
For a friend . . . when you're beaten, sick and blue
And the world's all wrong, for he won't care
If you break and cry, or grouch and swear,
For he'll let you know as he licks your hands
That he's downright sorry . . . and understands.

.   .   .   .

A long low shelf of teak will hold
My best-loved books in leather and gold
While magazines lie on a bowlegged stand
In a polyglot mixture close at hand.

.   .   .   .

On the mantelpiece I'll have a place
For a little mud god with a painted face
That was given to me . . . oh, long ago
By a Philippine maid in Olongapo.

.   .   .   .

And there where the shadows fall I've planned
To have a magnificent Concert-Grand
With polished wood and ivory keys

For wild discordant rhapsodies,
For wailing minor Hindu songs,
For Chinese chants with clanging gongs,
For flippant jazz and for lullabies
For moody things that I'll improvise
To play the long gray dusk away
And bid good-bye to another day.

Pictures . . . I think I'll have but three;
One, in oil, of a wind-swept sea
With the flying scud and the waves whipped white . . .
(I know the chap who can paint it right)
In lapis blue and a deep jade green . . .
A great big smashing fine marine
That'll make you feel the spray in your face.
I'll hang it over my fireplace.

The second picture . . . a freakish thing . . .
Is gaudy and bright as a macaw's wing,
An impressionistic smear called "Sin,"
A nude on a striped zebra skin
By a Danish girl I knew in France.
My respectable friends will look askance
At the purple eyes and the scarlet hair,
At the pallid face and the evil stare
Of the sinister beautiful vampire face.
I shouldn't have it about the place
But I like . . . while I loathe . . . the beastly thing
And that's the way that one feels about sin.

The picture I love the best of all
Will hang alone on my study wall
Where the sunset's glow and the moon's cold gleam
Will fall on the face and make it seem
That the eyes in the picture are meeting mine,
That the lips are curved in the fine sweet line

Of that wistful, tender, provocative smile
That has stirred my heart for a wondrous while.
It's a sketch of the girl who loved too well
To tie me down to that bit of Hell
That a drifter knows when he finds he's held
By the soft strong chains that passions weld.

It was best for her and for me, I know,
That she measured my love and bade me go
For we both have our great illusion yet
Unsoiled, unspoiled by a vain regret.
I won't deny that it makes me sad
To know that I've missed what I might have had.
It's a clean sweet memory, quite apart,
And I've been faithful . . . in my heart.

.   .   .   .

The beams of my house will be fragrant wood
That once in a teeming jungle stood
As a proud tall tree where the leopards couched
And the parrot screamed and the black men crouched.
The roof must have a rakish dip
To shadowy eaves where the rain can drip
In a damp, persistent tuneful way;
It's a cheerful sound on a gloomy day.
And I want a shingle loose somewhere
To wail like a banshee in despair
When the wind is high and the storm-gods race
And I am snug by my fireplace.

.   .   .   .

I'll have a cook that I'll name Oh Joy,
A sleek, fat, yellow-faced China boy
Who can roast a pig or mix a drink,
(you can't improve on a slant-eyed Chink).
On the gray-stone hearth there'll be a mat

For a scrappy, swaggering yellow cat
With a war-scarred face from a hundred fights
With neighbors' cats on moonlight nights.
A wise old Tom who can hold his own
And make my dogs let him alone.

. . . . .

Pewter and bronze and hammered brass,
Old carved wood and gleaming glass,
Candles in polychrome candlesticks
And peasant lamps in floating wicks,
Dragons in silk on a Mandarin suit
In a chest that is filled with vagabond-loot.
All of the beautiful useless things
That a vagabond's aimless drifting brings.
. . . Then when my house is all complete
I'll stretch me out on the window seat
With a favorite book and a cigarette
And a long cool drink that Oh Joy will get
And I'll look about at my bachelor-nest
While the sun goes zooming down the west
And the hot gold light will fall on my face
And make me think of some heathen place
That I've failed to see . . . that I've missed some
    way . . .
A place that I'd planned to find some day,
And I'll feel the lure of it drawing me.
Oh damn! I know what the end will be.
I'll go. And my house will fall away
While the mice by night and the moths by day
Will nibble the covers off all my books
And the spiders weave in the shadowed nooks
And my dogs . . . I'll see that they have a home
While I follow the sun, while I drift and roam
To the ends of the earth like a chip on the stream,
Like a straw on the wind, like a vagrant dream,
And the thought will strike with a swift sharp pain

That I probably never will build again
This house that I'll have in some far day.
Well . . . it's just a dream-house anyway.
                                        —Don Blanding.

SURVIVAL

A thousand years from this tonight
    When Orion climbs the sky,
The same swift snow will still the roofs,
    The same mad stars run by.

And who will know of China's war,
    Or poison gas in Spain?
The dead . . . they'll be forgotten, lost,
    Whether they lose or gain.

Of all the brilliant strategies
    Of war-lords now alive,
Perhaps a Chinese iris vase
    Of porcelain, may survive . . .

Perhaps a prayer, perhaps a song,
    Fashioned of love and tears,
But only beauty . . . only truth
    Will last a thousand years.
                                —Margaret Moore Meuttman.

7. CHARGE

Charge

>>><<<

THE STRUGGLE

Did you ever want to take your two bare hands,
  And choke out of the world your big success?
Beat, torn fists bleeding, pathways rugged, grand,
  By sheer brute strength and bigness, nothing less?
So at the last, triumphant, battered, strong,
  You might gaze down on what you choked and beat,
And say, "Ah, world, you've wrought to do me wrong;
  And thus have I accepted my defeat."

Have you ever dreamed of virile deeds, and vast,
  And then come back from dreams with wobbly knees,
To find your way (the braver vision past),
  By picking meekly at typewriter keys;
By bending o'er a ledger, day by day,
  By some machine-like drudging? No great woe
To grapple with. Slow, painful is the way,
  And still, the bravest fight and conquer so.
                              —Miriam Teichner.

CO-OPERATION

It ain't the guns nor armament,
  Nor funds that they can pay,
But the close co-operation,
  That makes them win the day.

It ain't the individual,
  Nor the army as a whole,
But the everlasting team-work
  Of every bloomin' soul.
                      —J. Mason Knox.

155

OUTWITTED

He drew a circle that shut me out—
Heretic, rebel, a thing to flout.
But Love and I had the wit to win:
We drew a circle that took him in!
                        —Edwin Markham.

THE INSULTING LETTER

Thanks for that insult.—I had too much peace:
    In the stone tavern down in yonder vale
    For a brief space too much of cakes and ale;
Too much of laughter. An ignoble ease
Had lured me from my vows and destinies.
    I had forgot the torrent and the gale,
    The cliff, the sunrise, and the forest trail,
And how I throve by nature but with these.

Thanks for that insult.—For it was your pen
Stirred the old blood and made me man again.
    And crushing your letter with all thought of you,
Inviolate will and fiery dream, I rose;
    Struck for the mountains, put my business through,
And stood victorious over larger foes.
                        —William Ellery Leonard.

YOU CAN—IF YOU THINK YOU CAN

If you think you are beaten; you are;
    If you think that you dare not, you don't;
If you'd like to win, but think you can't
    It's almost a "cinch" you won't.
If you think you'll lose, you've lost,
    For out in the world you find
Success begins with a fellow's will—
    It's all in the state of mind.

Fully many a race is lost
   Ere even a step is run,
And many a coward fails
   Ere even his work's begun,
Think big, and your deeds will grow,
   Think small, and you'll fall behind,
Think that you can, and you will—
   It's all in the state of mind.

If you think you're outclassed, you are;
   You've got to think high to rise;
You've got to be sure of yourself before
   You can ever win a prize.
Life's battles don't always go
   To the stronger or faster man,
But soon or late the man who wins
   Is the fellow who thinks he can.

                  —Unknown.

DON'T QUIT

When things go wrong, as they sometimes will,
When the road you're trudging seems all uphill,
When the funds are low, and the debts are high,
And you want to smile, but you have to sigh,
When care is pressing you down a bit,
Rest, if you must, but don't you quit!

Life is queer with twists and turns,
As everyone of us sometimes learns,
And many a failure turns about
When he might have won had he stuck it out.
Don't give up, though the pace seems slow,
You might succeed with another blow.
Often the goal is nearer than seems, to a faint
   and faltering man,
Often the struggler has given up

When he might have won the victor's cup and learned
Too late, when the night slipped down,
How close he was to the golden crown.

Success is failure turned inside out,
The silver tint on the cloud of doubt!
You never can tell how close you are,
You might be near, when it seems so far.
So stick to the fight when you're hardest hit:
It's when things are the worst that
You must not quit!

—Unknown.

WORTH WHILE

It's easy enough to be pleasant
    When life flows by like a song
But the man worth while is the one who will smile,
    When everything goes dead wrong.
For the test of the heart is trouble
    And it always comes with the years,
And the smile that is worth the praises of earth
    Is the smile that shines through tears.

It is easy enough to be prudent,
    When nothing tempts you to stray,
When without or within no voice of sin
    Is luring your soul away;
But it is only a negative virtue
    Until it is tried by fire,
And the life that is worth the honor on earth,
    Is the one that resists desire.

By the cynic, the sad, and the fallen,
    Who had no strength for the strife
The world's highway is cumbered today;
    They make up the sum of life.

But the virtue that conquers passion,
  And the sorrow that hides a smile,
It is these that are worth the homage on earth
  For we find them but once in a while.
                              —Ella Wheeler Wilcox.

DO YOU FEAR THE WIND?

Do you fear the force of the wind,
  The slash of the rain?
Go face them and fight them,
  Be savage again.
Go hungry and cold like the wolf,
  Go wade like the crane:
The palms of your hands will thicken,
  The skin of your cheek will tan,
You'll grow ragged and weary and swarthy,
  But you'll walk like a man!
                              —Hamlin Garland.

PREPAREDNESS

For all your days prepare,
  And meet them ever alike:
When you are the anvil, bear—
  When you are the hammer, strike.
                              —Edwin Markham.

A HOPEFUL BROTHER

Ef you ask him, day or night,
When the worl' warn't runnin' right,
"Anything that's good in sight?"
This is allus what he'd say,
In his uncomplainin' way—
  "Well, I'm hopin'."

When the winter days waz nigh,
An' the clouds froze in the sky,

Never sot him down to sigh.
But, still singin' on his way,
He'd stop long enough to say—
"Well, I'm hopin'."

Dyin', asked of him that night
(Sperrit waitin' fer its flight),
"Brother, air yer prospec's bright?"
An'—last words they heard him say,
In the ol', sweet, cheerful way—
"Well, I'm hopin'."
—Frank L. Stanton.

KEEP ON KEEPIN' ON

If the day looks kinder gloomy
    And your chances kinder slim,
If the situation's puzzlin'
    And the prospect's awful grim,
If perplexities keep pressin'
    Till hope is nearly gone,
Just bristle up and grit your teeth
    And keep on keepin' on.

Frettin' never wins a fight
    And fumin' never pays;
There ain't no use in broodin'
    In these pessimistic ways;
Smile just kinder cheerfully
    Though hope is nearly gone,
And bristle up and grit your teeth
    And keep on keepin' on.

There ain't no use in growlin
    And grumblin' all the time,
When music's ringin' everywhere
    And everything's a rhyme.

Just keep on smilin' cheerfully
　　If hope is nearly gone,
And bristle up and grit your teeth
　　And keep on keepin' on.
　　　　　　　　　　—Unknown.

STUPIDITY

I said you'd better go away
　　And forget you ever knew me,
But women say such funny things
　　I thought you'd see right through me!
　　　　　　　　—Mildred M. Hott.

A POOR UNFORTUNATE

His hoss went dead an' his mule went lame;
He lost six cows in a poker game;
A harricane came on a summer's day,
An' carried the house whar' he lived away;
Then a airthquake come when that wuz gone,
An' swallered the lan' that the house stood on!
An' the tax collector, he come roun'
An' charged him up fer the hole in the groun'!
An' the city marshal—he come in view
An' said he wanted his street tax, too!

Did he moan an' sigh? Did he set an' cry
An' cuss the harricane sweepin' by?
Did he grieve that his ol' friends failed to call
When the airthquake come an' swallered all?
Never a word o' blame he said,
With all them troubles on top his head!
Not him. . . . He clumb to the top o' the hill—
Whar' standin' room wuz left him still,
An', barin' his head, here's what he said:
"I reckon it's time to git up an' git;
But, Lord, I hain't had the measels yit!"
　　　　　　　　　—Frank L. Stanton.

THE QUITTER

When you're lost in the wild and you're scared as a child,
  And death looks you bang in the eye;
And you're sore as a boil, it's according to Hoyle
  To cock your revolver and die.
But the code of a man says fight all you can,
  And self-dissolution is barred;
In hunger and woe, oh it's easy to blow—
  It's the hell served for breakfast that's hard.

You're sick of the game? Well now, that's a shame!
  You're young and you're brave and you're bright,
You've had a raw deal, I know, but don't squeal.
  Buck up, do your damnedest and fight!
It's the plugging away that will win you the day,
  So don't be a piker, old pard;
Just draw on your grit; it's so easy to quit—
  It's the keeping your chin up that's hard.

It's easy to cry that you're beaten and die,
  It's easy to crawfish and crawl,
But to fight and to fight when hope's out of sight,
  Why, that's the best game of them all.
And though you come out of each grueling bout,
  All broken and beaten and scarred—
Just have one more try. It's dead easy to die,
  It's keeping on living that's hard.
                              —Robert W. Service.

UNSUBDUED

I have hoped, I have planned, I have striven,
  To the will I have added the deed;
The best that was in me I've given,
  I have prayed, but the gods would not heed.

I have dared and reached only disaster,
    I have battled and broken my lance;
I am bruised by a pitiless master
    That the weak and the timid call Chance.

I am old, I am bent, I am cheated
    Of all that Youth urged me to win;
But name me not with the defeated,
    To-morrow again, I begin.
                  —S. E. Kiser.

PRAYER FOR THE NEW YEAR

Great Power that set a little decency alight
    Within this mass of flesh and bone I call myself,
Hear now the prayer I make for this new year to come.

I ask not now for wisdom, for I find
    I do not use the little that I have;
Nor do I ask for power, for I fear
    The brute in me, that uses power as a club;
Nor riches, for I know full well that I
    Receive all that I earn, and maybe more.
I asked for these things once, in years gone by,
    And, in a measure, they have all been mine;
Each gift I craved was granted unto me
    As all things that we crave are granted from your
       store—
But if you have a face, Great Power, I know you smiled
    As from that store you gave the thing I craved,
For well you knew it would not fill my heart
    Nor make for beauty in my stupid hands.
So now, with clearer vision and a humbler heart
    I come to beg for that one precious boon—

Which is, I think, the greatest gift of all—
    Help me to be kind!
Help me be kind in motive and in deed,
    Help me be kind in my most secret thought,
In every touch I make on other lives,
    In every contact which they press on me.
Cleanse all the stinging rancor from my wit,
    Purge me of envy, greed and smug self-righteousness.
Make me remember only my own weakness, my own
        sin,
    When fools and sinners ask some boon of me.
Help me be kind!
    Not with the patronizing pity that's a lash
At self-respect, nor with a pride
    That crushes those who show their need to me,
But with the constant knowledge that whate'er I have
    Of strength or money, wit or cleverness,
Belongs to them as much as it belongs to me.
    For all of it has come from out your store,
And those who give or take are brothers in your sight.
    And when I meet with scorn and ridicule,
When I am tricked by my own malice or stupidity
    And stand ashamed, besmirched before the sneering
        eyes of men,
Help me to keep my spirit sweet in that dark hour,
    Hold back my temper, make me tolerant and sane
To those that hurt me, as to those that I might hurt
    Help me be kind!

Great Power, who made me from the common clay,
    Yet breathed into that clay a flash of godlike fire,
Breathe now again, to light me through the year, and
        warm
    My cold, hard spirit with that pure white ray of your
        own kindness.
                                        —Elsie Robinson.

SO IS HE MADE

Beneath the hill, athwart the stream
The mind of man pursues its dream,

Burrowing, building to erase
Nature from earth's eternal face,

To seal her mouth and close her eyes
With what he may himself devise.

The temporal shadow on his heart
His stubborn will must thrust apart—

The everlasting land and seed
The waiting furrow with his need.

With hands no larger than a leaf
He brings a forest down to grief,

Troubles the air with metal wings,
And prowls between the roots of things.

Clearly he sees the strength of stone
In mountains, yet he'll match his bone

Against it, and the mountains bend
Their terrible backs to shape his end.

.   .   .   .

Whatever he may hew or hack
He knows that time will take it back,

That his swift mind may not outrun
Earth's patient cycle round the sun.

And yet so urgent is he made,
So transient and so unafraid,

Who now before our mortal eyes
Conquers the deathless thing and dies.
                              —Sarah Litsey.

I HAVE A RENDEZVOUS WITH DEATH

I have a rendezvous with Death
At some disputed barricade,
When Spring comes round with rustling shade
And apple-blossoms fill the air—
I have a rendezvous with Death
When Spring brings back blue days and fair.

It may be he shall take my hand
And lead me into his dark land
And close my eyes and quench my breath—
It may be I shall pass him still.
I have a rendezvous with Death
On some scarred slope of battered hill,
And the first meadow-flowers appear.

God knows 'twere better to be deep
Pillowed in silk and scented down,
Where Love throbs out in blissful sleep,
Pulse nigh to pulse, and breath to breath,
Where hushed awakenings are dear. . . .
But I've a rendezvous with Death
At midnight in some flaming town,
When Spring trips north again this year,
And I to my pledged word am true,
I shall not fail that rendezvous.
                              —Alan Seeger.

LOST CITY

We shall build it again though it caves in,
  And the ramparts fall where the moss is,
  And the draw-bridge no horseman crosses
Lets the dusk and the wind and the waves in.

We shall build it with hills and with hollows,
  And small slopes where vineyards are sprawling,
  And a wall that crumbles in falling,
And a river nobody follows.

Through the gateways we'll see to the centre
  Where fountains are playing, and flowers
  Run a flame up the twilit towers
Of the city we never shall enter.

And the wind will die down in the streamers,
  And the spires will fall with the night-fall;
  But a door will open . . . a light fall
On a street that is peopled with dreamers.
                    —Marion Strobel.

YOUTH

We are the militant, the undefeated, Youth!
  Out of the wreckage of our world today
We climb, the eager seekers after truth,
  And nothing can detain us on our way.
The sun still shines, the hills are there to climb,
  The stars lead out, and life is ours to live;
Our hearts are high; we came for such a time,
  And we have much to offer, much to give.

There are the undreamed cities yet to build;
  Great airports planned for riders of the skies;

Mines to be sunk, and wide fields to be tilled;
  Beneath our hands our own home walls will rise:
Love will be ours, young women and young men
  Walking the highways of the earth to make
The old defeated world take heart again;
  Make laughter certain for our childrens' sake.
                              —Grace Noll Crowell.

-»×«-

For forms of government let fools contest;
Whate'er is best administer'd is best:
For modes of faith let graceless zealots fight;
His can't be wrong whose life is in the right.
In faith and hope the world will disagree,
But all mankind's concern is charity:
All must be false that thwart this one great end;
And all of God, that bless mankind or mend.
                              —Alexander Pope.

SOME FAITH AT ANY COST

No vision and you perish;
  No ideal, and you're lost;
Your heart must ever cherish
  Some faith at any cost.

Some hope, some dream to cling to,
  Some rainbow in the sky,
Some melody to sing to,
  Some service that is high.
                  —Harriet du Autermont.

WHICH ARE YOU?

I watched them tearing a building down,
A gang of men in a busy town;
With a ho-heave-ho and a lusty yell
They swung a beam and the sidewalk fell.

I asked the foreman: "Are these men skilled,
And the men you'd hire if you had to build?"
He gave a laugh and said: "No indeed!
Just common labor is all I need.
I can easily wreck in a day or two
What builders have taken a year to do!"

And I thought to myself as I went my way,
Which of these roles have I tried to play?
Am I a builder who works with care,
Measuring life by the rule and square?
Am I shaping my deeds to a well-made plan,
Patiently doing the best I can?
Or am I a wrecker, who walks the town,
Content with the labor of tearing down?

—Unknown.

WINGS

Within man's heart is ever the longing to fly:
    The inherent upward reaching toward the light,
The eternal call of the heart for the arching sky,
    The tug of invisible wings for a headlong flight—
These have striven within him, and will strive
    As long as one golden eagle, strong and free
Stretches its sun-tipped wings, alert, alive,
    And climbs to the borderland of eternity.

To be one with the wind in its far-flung heady race,
    To be one with the stars, one with the sun as it
        swings
Upon its outbound course, to fly with the grace
    Of the wildest bird! For "wings, wings, wings,"
Men have cried, until they found them at last. . . .
    Dear God,
    Steady the wings as they lift these days from the sod.
            —Grace Noll Crowell.

A SONG OF TOIL

America is working! Once again
   There is the sound of labor in the land.
Flame-bright the forges light the ending dark,
   And tasks begin for every reaching hand.
There is the ring of anvils in the night,
   The swing of axes, march of workers' feet,
And steel flows molten, shining as a dream—
   Now we have learned shrill whistles may be sweet!

Triumphantly the flag waves high and free
   Above the smoke where industry begins,
Above the busyness of shops and stores,
   Above the hearts purged clean of idle sins.
Oh, always it is good to have a task,
   The plan of life must grant some work to men.
So let the bugles play, the deep drums throb,
   America has gone to work again!
                —Helen Welshimer.

WORK

Let me but do my work from day to day,
   In field or forest, at the desk or loom,
   In roaring market-place or tranquil room;
Let me but find it in my heart to say,
When vagrant wishes beckon me astray,
   "This is my work; my blessing, not my doom;
   Of all who live, I am the one by whom
This work can best be done in the right way."

Then shall I see it not too great, nor small,
   To suit my spirit and to prove my powers;
   Then shall I cheerful greet the laboring hours,
And cheerful turn, when the long shadows fall
At eventide, to play and love and rest,
Because I know for me my work is best.
                —Henry van Dyke.

THE LAY OF THE LAST MINSTREL

Breathes there the man with soul so dead,
Who never to himself hath said,
This is my own, my native land!
Whose heart hath ne'er within him burn'd
As home his footsteps he hath turned
From wandering on a foreign strand!
If such there breathe, go, mark him well!
For him no minstrel raptures swell;
High though his titles, proud his name,
Boundless his wealth as wish can claim;
Despite those titles, power, and pelf,
The wretch, concentred all in self,
Living, shall forfeit fair renown,
And, doubly dying, shall go down
To the vile dust from whence he sprung,
Unwept, unhonour'd, and unsung.

—Sir Walter Scott.

GROWTH

Toward what far end
I move, I do not know,
And just as long as I may go
On with the trend
Of things, I do not care—

Learning all that I can grasp
At any time and anywhere,
Doing what is to be done,
From sun to sun—
Accepting gratefully the clasp
Of any joy, and if pain comes,
To try to bear it gallantly
In mind and heart,

For either happiness or sorrow
Is each a part
Of growing toward a finer morrow—

For growing through both good and ill
Means progress—never standing still!
                              —Peter A. Lea.

MY BROTHER AND I STAND IN THE DARK

I lean my head against the wood
Of a mighty elm which stood
Before I was as much as a thought
And will be standing when I am not,
The wide-hung branches of the tree
Make a small world over me,
The stars, high millions of miles above,
Go over scornfully, but love
Covers me from their cold scorn
And makes me glad that I was born.

My brother and I stand in the dark
Side by side, and if I hark,
I can hear him praising deep
The race of men and trees who keep
Coming up from the senseless turf
And who some day will warm the surf
Of the farthest stars with great
Brotherhood and break the gate
Beyond the stars and find there room
For limbs and leaves to lift and bloom
Beyond the reach of day and night
With law of living for their light.
                    —Robert P. Tristram Coffin.

EACH IN HIS OWN TONGUE

A fire-mist and a planet,—
  A crystal and a cell,—
A jellyfish and a saurian,
  And caves where cave-men dwell;
Then a sense of law and beauty,
  And a face turned from the clod,—
Some call it Evolution,
  And others call it God.

A haze on the far horizon,
  The infinite, tender sky,
The ripe, rich tints of the cornfields,
  And the wild geese sailing high,—
And all over upland and lowland
  The charm of the goldenrod,—
Some of us call it Autumn,
  And others call it God.

Like tides on a crescent sea-beach,
  When the moon is new and thin,
Into our hearts high yearnings
  Come welling and surging in,—
Come from the mystic ocean,
  Whose rim no foot has trod,—
Some of us call it Longing,
  And others call it God.

A picket frozen on duty,—
  A mother starved for her brood,—
Socrates drinking the hemlock
  And Jesus on the rood;

And millions who, humble and nameless,
   The straight, hard pathway plod,—
Some call it Consecration,
   And others call it God.
              —William Herbert Carruth.

WHEN I HEARD THE LEARN'D ASTRONOMER

When I heard the learn'd astronomer,
When the proofs, the figures, were ranged in columns
   before me,
When I was shown the charts and diagrams, to add,
   divide, and measure them,
When I, sitting, heard the astronomer where he lectured
   with much applause in the lecture-room,
How soon unaccountable I became tired and sick,
Till rising and gliding out I wander'd off by myself,
In the mystical moist night-air, and from time to time,
Look'd up in perfect silence at the stars.
              —Walt Whitman.

FOR A MATERIALIST

I

I know your barren belief—that a rose will grow
   From what was once the miracle of a man;
That only in this way shall we thwart the grave;
   Believe, my friend, and be satisfied, if you can.

But I have a mystical hunger, so great and intense
   That only Almighty God with a purpose would fill
My fragile shell with its poignant immensity—
   A hunger to find, emerging from death, that I still
Am the sum of myself! myself, to aspire and climb
Some farther and undreamed slope of the range of Time.

I have faith that I shall. Is a rose worth the patience of
   Him

Who evolved through the aeons a man and endowed
    him with soul?
Would He who created the splendor of spirit and mind
    Envisage a sweet-scented waft as its trivial goal?

II

You say that the soul is forever commingled with matter,
    That it lives since the body lives and dies when that
        dies,
That it feels and thinks with the flesh and perceives
    creations
    With the body's eyes.

The two are knit, I know, for the length of a lifetime;
But tell me—have you not seen a spirit unfold
Its beauty and grow more vital although the body
             Was faded and old?
Whence this splendor apart, this effervescence,
This gaining in strength through the years that the end
    can show,
If it depend so wholly on forces receding,
             On sap running low?
The body may be assailed by the frosts of winter
And the spirit be steeped in the sunniness of May;
Why shall it not maintain, when matter has crumbled,
             Its separate way?

III

A dusty dissolution! So Death means
    No more than this dry thing to you—no more.
Oh, I am one who confidently gleans
    A rich surmise from shadows cast before;
From this insatiate seeking, this sublime
    Persistence of man's soul, intent to find
The shining Core from which the rays of Time
    And Life proceed; from this assault of mind,

The strong, well tempered weapon which man brings
    To all adventure, his Excalibar
With which in his eternal questionings
    He storms for answers earth and sea and star!
Would any God who breathes in us such need
    And power to learn of Him, who lets us look
Upon some pages freely, bid us read
    The preface only—and then shut the book?

                              —Adelaide Love.

A NOISELESS, PATIENT SPIDER

A noiseless, patient spider,
I marked, where, on a little promontory, it stood isolated;
Marked how, to explore the vacant, vast surrounding,
It launched forth filament, filament, filament, out of
    itself;
Ever unreeling them—ever tirelessly speeding them.

And you, O my soul, where you stand,
Surrounded, surrounded, in measureless oceans of space,
Ceaselessly musing, venturing, throwing,—seeking the
    spheres, to connect them;
Till the bridge you will need, be formed—till the
    ductile anchor hold;
Till the gossamer thread you fling, catch somewhere, O
    my Soul.

                              —Walt Whitman.

MY CREED

I would be true, for there are those who trust me;
    I would be pure, for there are those who care;
I would be strong, for there is much to suffer;
    I would be brave, for there is much to dare.

I would be friend of all—the foe, the friendless;
  I would be giving and forget the gift;
I would be humble, for I know my weakness;
  I would look up—and laugh—and love—and lift.
                    —Howard Arnold Walter.

THE WAYS

To every man there openeth
A Way, and Ways, and a Way.
And the High Soul climbs the High Way,
  And the Low Soul gropes the Low,
And in between, on the misty flats,
  The rest drift to and fro.
But to every man there openeth
  A High Way, and a Low.
And every man decideth
  The Way his soul shall go.
                    —John Oxenham.

THE WOMAN WHO UNDERSTANDS

Somewhere she waits to make you win, your soul in her
  firm, white hands—
Somewhere the gods have made for you, the Woman Who
  Understands!

As the tide went out she found him
  Lashed to a spar of Despair,
The wreck of his Ship around him—
  The wreck of his Dreams in the air;
Found him and loved him and gathered
  The soul of him close to her heart—
The soul that had sailed an uncharted sea,
The soul that had sought to win and be free—
  The soul of which she was part!
    And there in the dusk she cried to the man,
    "Win your battle—you can, you can!"

Broken by Fate, unrelenting,
  Scarred by the lashings of Chance;
Bitter his heart—unrepenting—
  Hardened by Circumstance;
Shadowed by Failure ever,
  Cursing, he would have died,
But the touch of her hand, her strong warm hand,
And her love of his soul, took full command,
  Just at the turn of the tide!
    Standing beside him, filled with trust,
    "Win!" she whispered, "you must, you must!"

Helping and loving and guiding,
  Urging when that were best,
Holding her fears in hiding
  Deep in her quiet breast;
This is the woman who kept him
  True to his standards lost,
When, tossed in the storm and stress of strife,
He thought himself through with the game of life
  And ready to pay the cost.
    Watching and guarding, whispering still,
    "Win you can—and you will, you will!"

This is the story of ages,
  This is the Woman's way;
Wiser than seers or sages,
  Lifting us day by day;
Facing all things with a courage
  Nothing can daunt or dim,
Treading Life's path, wherever it leads—
Lined with flowers or choked with weeds,
  But ever with him—with him!
    Guidon—comrade—golden spur—
    The men who win are helped by her!

Somewhere she waits, strong in belief, your soul in her
firm, white hands:
Thank well the gods, when she comes to you—the Woman
Who Understands!

       —Everard Jack Appleton.

YOU HAVE TO BELIEVE

You have to believe in happiness,
 Or happiness never comes.
I know that a bird chirps none the less
 When all that he finds is crumbs.
You have to believe the buds will blow
Believe in the grass in the days of snow;
 Ah, that's the reason a bird can sing—
 On his darkest day he believes in Spring.

You have to believe in happiness—
 It isn't an outward thing.
The Spring never makes the song, I guess,
 As much as the song the Spring.
Aye, many a heart could find content
If it saw the joy on the road it went
 The joy ahead when it had to grieve—
 For the joy is there—but you have to believe.

       —Douglas Malloch.

COURAGE

Courage is the price that Life exacts for granting peace,
The soul that knows it not
Knows no release from little things:

Knows not the livid loneliness of fear,
Nor mountain heights where bitter joy can hear
The sound of wings.

How can Life grant us boon of living, compensate
For dull gray ugliness and pregnant hate
Unless we dare

The soul's dominion? Each time we make a choice, we pay
With courage to behold resistless day,
And count it fair.

—Amelia Earhart.

OPPORTUNITY

This I beheld, or dreamed it in a dream:—
There spread a cloud of dust along a plain;
And underneath the cloud, or in it, raged
A furious battle, and men yelled, and swords
Shocked upon swords and shields. A prince's banner
Wavered, then staggered backward, hemmed by foes.
A craven hung along the battle's edge,
And thought, "Had I a sword of keener steel—
That blue blade that the king's son bears,—but this
Blunt thing—!" he snapt and flung it from his hand,
And lowering crept away and left the field.
Then came the king's son, wounded, sore bestead,
And weaponless, and saw the broken sword,
Hilt-buried in the dry and trodden sand,
And ran and snatched it, and with battle-shout
Lifted afresh he hewed his enemy down,
And saved a great cause that heroic day.

—Edward Rowland Sill.

DUTY

So nigh is grandeur to our dust,
    So near is God to man,
When duty whispers low, *Thou must*,
    The youth replies, *I can*.

—Ralph Waldo Emerson.

MY PRAYER

God let me live each lovely day,
   So I may know, that come what may:
I've done my best, to live the way,
   You want me to.

Forgive me if I do not pray,
   In church on every Sabbath day;
The ultra sanctimonious way,
   As some folks do.

Just let me know if I should stray,
   That I may stop along the way;
At any time of night or day,
   And talk to You.

               —Elsie Janis.

TRUTH AT LAST

Does a man ever give up hope, I wonder,—
Face the grim fact, seeing it clear as day?
When Bennen saw the snow slip, heard its thunder
Low, louder, roaring round him, felt the speed
Grow swifter as the avalanche hurled downward,
Did he for just one heart-throb—did he indeed
Know with all certainty, as they swept onward,
There was the end, where the crag dropped away?
Or did he think, even till they plunged and fell,
Some miracle would stop them? Nay, they tell
That he turned round, face forward, calm and pale,
Stretching his arms out toward his native vale
As if in mute, unspeakable farewell,
And so went down.—'Tis something, if at last,
Though only for a flash, a man may see
Clear-eyed the future as he sees the past,
From doubt, or fear, or hope's illusion free.

               —Edward Rowland Sill.

➤➤✕⤙⤙

Sound, sound the clarion, fill the fife!
　To all the sensual world proclaim,
One crowded hour of glorious life
　Is worth an age without a name
　　　　　　　　—Sir Walter Scott.

➤➤✕⤙⤙

Here is a toast that I want to drink,
　To a fellow I'll never know,
To the fellow who's going to take my place
　When it's time for me to go,
I've wondered what kind of a chap he'll be
　And I've wished I could take his hand,
Just to whisper, "I wish you well, old man,"
　In a way that he'd understand.
I'd like to give him the cheering word
　That I've longed at times to hear;
I'd like to give him the warm hand clasp
　When never a friend seemed near.
I've earned my knowledge by sheer hard work
　And I wish I could pass it on
To the fellow who'll come and take my place
　Some day when I am gone.

Will he see the sad mistakes I've made
　And note the battles lost?
Will he ever guess the tears they caused,
　Or the heartaches which they cost?
Will he gaze through failure and fruitless toil
　To the underlying plan,
And catch a glimpse of the real interest,
　And the heart of the vanished man?
I dare to hope he may pause someday
　As he toils where I have wrought;
And gain some strength from his weary task
　From the battles which I have fought.

But I've only the task itself to leave
  With the cares for him to face.
And never a cheering word may speak
  To the fellow who'll take my place.

Then here's to your health, Old Chap, I drink
  As a bridegroom to his bride;
I leave an unfinished task for you,
  But God knows I have tried.
I've dreamed my dreams, as all men do;
  Some of those dreams came true,
And my prayer today is that all these dreams
  May be realized by you.
And we'll meet someday, in the Great Unknown,
  Out of the realm of space.
You'll know my clasp, as I take your hand
  And gaze in your tired face.
Then all our hopes will be realized
  In the light of the new dawn,
So I'm drinking your health, and success, Old Chap,
  Who takes my place when I'm gone.
               —Dr. Walter Lathrop.

8. FIRE

Fire

EVERY hour in every life is filled with the annoying necessity of decision. Which shall we do—this or that? Which road shall we take—this one or that one. "Make up your mind! Which do you want?" It is the demand for action . . . Fire! . . . the choice. We cannot ever escape it long.

Yet some of the most important adventures in life are influenced, if not decided, by apparently trivial things. I missed a train one night that three hours later was badly wrecked. The coach in which I would have been riding was almost completely destroyed. At every corner we decide which side of the street to take, never knowing how different life would be if we crossed the avenue. One "no" in place of a "yes" can completely change a whole life. I have long been interested in the frequency with which poetry seems to play a part in some of life's most important decisions. There are enough examples in my files to fill a set of books. Here are a few of the stories and, though they are not so bizarre as many I have received, they are interesting because they are typical, and of course are actual experiences as told by the people themselves.

❯❯❯❮❮❮

"Thinking back on poetry which has influenced my life, I remember the months before my wedding. My generation of professional women believed marriage interfered with their 'careers'—when, as, and if. Divorce statistics were soaring—and scaring. All the weight of

187

evidence, according to my friends, piled up against my marrying.

"My newspaper, *The Evening World*, sent me to interview the English poet, Wilfrid Wilson Gibson. Looking through a volume of his poems, I came upon the eight lines he calls 'Marriage.'

> Going my way of old,
>   Contented more or less,
> I dreamt not life could hold
>   Such happiness.
>
> I dreamt not that love's way
>   Could keep the golden height
> Day after happy day,
>   Night after night.

"I learned these lines literally by heart, and they confirmed my private conviction of what marriage can mean. In the twenty-five years since I read Gibson's poem I have found it told the simple truth about my own marriage to Sidney Walter Dean—who writes better books than I do, yet who likes mine.

Sincerely yours,
Marguerite Mooers Marshall Dean."

->>><<<-

Here is what seems to be a most casual incident, yet it wholly determined the path of life of Richard F. Blyer, Minister of the First Congregational Church in Concord, New Hampshire:

"The moment is as vivid as the incidents of yesterday. I was eighteen and much distressed in mind as to what should be my life-work. An opportunity had presented itself to enter dramatic work. I had a 'mania' for 'acting' from my earliest days. In spite of all this I had a strong interest in the Christian ministry.

"In this general confusion of mind I stretched myself out on the living room couch—I reached for a copy of the New Testament—opened it at random and found myself reading words that I had never come upon to my knowledge.

"They were words in the First Letter to the Corinthians—the Fourth Chapter—the Seventh Verse:
'What has thou that thou hast not received and if thou hast received why dost thou glory as if thou hadst not received it.'

"There was something that struck me cold and then warm. The capital of my life—in whatever it consisted—was a divine award. It was to be so regarded and used to the very best of one's ability. The Christian Ministry seemed like the most fitting opportunity in which to invest the capital of my life. My decision was sealed."

->>|<<-

Here is a curious example of a poem that somehow has been lost completely, yet perhaps saved a life. Without knowing the name and address, which I could give you, take my word for it, the story is true!

"I worked for a handsome up-and-coming M.D. and was madly in love with him. Mind now, I say madly, with all meaning for that is very nearly where it landed me. He was caught up in the social whirl and I was left out or at home sitting forlornly by the telephone waiting for his call.

"This suspense did things to my power of reasoning. I don't know now why I did what I did, but no one ever does. Anyway, I wrote my mother a farewell note, stayed over late at the office, and was prepared to fling myself down eight floors to the ground.

"The phone rang and it was only a girl friend calling to read a poem to me which she said reminded her so much of the little Irish friend she was talking to. I cannot recall much of the poem and she didn't even keep it as it didn't seem so important to her. But it told of a girl with great courage in the face of many difficulties—how she smiled so much and kept faith with the best in herself.

"Well, I went straight home and found the note, destroyed it, and called my girlhood boy-friend who is now my husband. We have four babies and a nice marmalade business besides his good job in town."

Ten years ago I would have doubted that story. Five years ago I would have rationalized it . . . but having known so many similar experiences, now I don't question it . . . I just believe in the magic of poetry.

>>>><<<<

Here is a little story told me by Mrs. Elizabeth Mac-Gregor, which is complete in itself:

"Seven years ago I heard of a young English couple who had come to our United States. They had been here a short while when the husband was killed in an automobile accident. A month later the young mother gave birth to a tiny boy, but in giving it its life, she died. There were no living relatives, and the nurse and doctor said he would be placed in an orphan's home. What a shame! I needed a baby! I didn't have any! I had a nice home! I had an extra room! It could be made into a nursery! (I couldn't go out as often as I had. I would probably lose sleep when he cried or was sick. He would be extra work. He would need lots of things.) These things I thought, but then I read:

Take heed of this small child of earth;
    He is great: he hath in him God most high,
Children before their fleshly birth
    Are lights alive in the blue sky.

In our light, bitter world of wrongs
    They come; God gives us them awhile.

His speech is in their stammering tongue,
  And his forgiveness in their smile.

Their sweet light rests upon our eyes.
  Alas! Their right to joy is plain.
If they are hungry, Paradise
  Weeps, and if cold, Heaven thrills with pain.

The want that saps their sinless flower
  Speaks judgment on sin's ministers.
Man holds an angel in his power.
  Ah! deep in heaven what thunder stirs,

When God seeks out these tender things
  Whom in the shadow where we sleep
He sends us clothed about with wings
  And finds the ragged babes that weep!

"I made application for this baby, and got him for a
six-month period of probation and then we legally
adopted him.

"We love him as our own, but have told him we picked
him out of all the babies in the world, and adopted him
because he had no mother or father to love him. He
understands, and the other night when I was putting him
to bed, he said, 'When I die, I hope God will turn me
into a baby again, and if you are up in heaven, I will
pick *you* out for my *real mother*, for you are the only
mother I want.'

"That paid for all the work, all the trouble, all the
nights I stayed awake when he was small. Thank God
for babies, and thank God for poems!"

→>≻≪←

From Marion Colman of Anna Maria, Florida, came
this amusing little story of an episode in her life:
" 'A laght, a laght, a laght, a laght,' droned the youthful mountaineer at the Columbus Day chapel service.

'Hit grew, a storrlit flaig unfurrled;
Hit grew to be Tahm's burrst of doane;
He gained a worrld: he gave thet worrld
Hit's graindest lesson. Own, sail Own.'

"This was merely one of a seemingly endless pro-
gression of chapel services, slightly better than some,
but soon forgotten in the on-coming rush of events in a
small school in the Southern Highlands.

"Some weeks later I was in a quandary about whether
or not to continue teaching in this school during the
second semester. I loved the rounded, corn-clad hills
and the sturdy mountain youngsters—even though they
were prone to tell me 'Ah cain't, Miss C,' whenever I
proposed anything new or different for chapel or classes.
But I was attempting a schedule beyond my capabilities,
and certain misunderstandings with my superiors made
it seem impossible to continue.

"I must have been praying about it one starry evening
as I walked out on the campus. Some people get such
wonderful guidance, I thought. They always know just
what to do. Why must I always grope along in the dark?

"Suddenly a lantern flashed along a distant pathway.
Then sprang to my mind the words:

A light, a light, a light, a light,

and as clearly as though they had been spoken:

Sail on, sail on, sail on and on.

"Could this be the answer I sought?

"I stayed. And many rewarding experiences convinced
me that the choice was decidedly right."

I know some people will say that Miss Colman rationalized her experience. Let them say it.

❧❧❧❧

Then read this . . . not as an example of decision . . .
but of the magic of poetry—quoting from another letter:

"The two persons concerned were deeply drawn to
each other. But one was not being frank and open as to
the facts of his life, and the barriers which lay between
them. At last he summoned all his courage and made a
clean breast of the matter. The other, the woman, was so
stunned by the revelation that a sense of utter lifeless-
ness, of detachment, and unreality enfolded her. Then
came these lines:

> After great pain, a formal feeling comes.
> The nerves sit, ceremonious, like tombs.

" 'A formal feeling . . . the nerves sit, ceremonious
. . . ' Then this was something that could happen . . .
it had happened before . . . someone else had felt this,
and had lived on.

"Calmly, she rose and suggested that they drink some
coffee. In a little while she and the man she loved were
discussing their situation, looking at it squarely. There
were no hysterics, no angry words, no regrets. There was
Emily Dickinson.

Signed,
'The Woman.' "

❧❧❧❧

But these are to be examples of "decisions," determined by poetry.

"Every young girl goes through stages of wanting to
become a school teacher, an actress, and a nurse, among
many other ambitions. While in the throes of adoles-
cence, I came upon 'With Hands That Are Holy.'

You, who uncurl the rumpled rose-leaf hands of little
passengers so lately come through dawn's pearl gate
with gold and agate bands, keep your own hands as pure
and tendersome.

And when some weary one slips out with day, hold fast his hand that he may stumble not the first few faltering steps the way, until he knows that God had not forgot.

"I knew then that I must become a nurse. Many times since then have I 'Uncurled rose-petal hands' and held tightly to restless hands of those about to depart on their last journey.

Reba A. Swicegood, R. N."

->>><<<-

There are other kinds of decisions we make and sometimes they are influenced by poetry too.

"It was after the war. My brother and his wife had married while in the last year of college. After graduating, they had fully intended leading a domestic life. They were reading Walt Whitman's 'Leaves of Grass' at the time, and then they came to his 'Song of the Open Road':

Afoot and light-hearted I take to the open road,
Healthy, free, the world before me,
The long brown path before me leading wherever I choose.
Henceforth I ask not good fortune, I myself am good fortune,
Henceforth I whimper no more, postpone no more, need nothing,
Done with indoor complaints, libraries, querulous criticism,
Strong and content I travel the open road.

"The poem so inspired them that it changed their future life for many years. They decided then and there to travel. Having very little money, they decided to hike. His wife carried a twenty-pound pack, he a thirty-five-pound pack, and in this way, over a period of about four years, they reached every state in the U.S.A.

My brother said that this experience taught him more than all the four years of his college education."

>>><<<

One of the most interesting examples of the direct influence of poetry on a decision I found in a letter from a Dorothy Wilson:

"Sometime ago I went on a vacation alone. I arrived late in the afternoon, terribly dirty and tired from a long train ride on the Erie, only to find that the place didn't look as I had pictured it, and I didn't like the room they had given me. It was very small and up on the top floor. There were an awful lot of people there and everyone seemed to know everyone else, so I also felt lonesome. That's an awful combination for the beginning of a vacation; tired, dirty, disgusted and lonesome. I was all set to go back home when a girl in the next room recited:

> Never say Die, say Damn!
> It isn't classic, it may be profane,
> But we mortals have need of it, time and again.
> And you'll find you'll recover
> From Fate's hardest slam
> If you never say Die, say Damn!

"Well, to make a long story short, I said 'Damn.' Got myself cleaned up and rested. That evening at the dance I was introduced to the young man who is now my husband. After that I wasn't in my room long enough for it to annoy me, so all my troubles were over and I had a grand time.

"We have been married now going on thirteen years, have a lovely son, aged seven, and are very happy. I have since bought a framed copy of this verse and it hangs in our hall. We call it 'Wilson's Motto.' I have often wondered just what my life would have been if Elsie (the girl who recited the poem) hadn't said it just then or if the walls had been thicker and I had gone home."

⇒»)«⇐

Here is a story just as it came to me.

"According to the weather forecast one afternoon in the spring of 1938, the day was bright and sunny with clear blue skies overhead, the trees bursting in bud and the crocus were in full bloom, so I was told. All these things were awakening to Mother Nature's beckoning. I could not feel this fancy of spring, for two weeks previous I was stricken blind. Within me rose a sense of utter uselessness, when through my radio someone in a soft soothing voice, as if he understood, was reading Milton's:

> When I consider how my light is spent
> Ere half my days, in this dark world and wide,
> And that one talent which is death to hide
> Lodged with me useless, though my soul more bent
> To serve therewith my Maker, and present
> My true account, lest he returning chide;
> 'Doth God exact day-labour, light denied?'
> I fondly ask. But Patience, to prevent
> That murmur, soon replies, 'God doth not need
> Either man's work or his own gifts. Who best
> Bear his mild yoke, they serve him best.
> His state is kingly; thousands at his bidding
> Speed, and post o'er land and ocean without rest;
> They also serve who only stand and wait.

"Over and over again I repeated that last line to myself. I waited, waited two long years, and the Lord served me. He lifted the veil of darkness and the next spring I saw the clear blue sky, the budding trees and picked the first crocus from our garden.

Alice Holmes."

-»>«-

If it weren't that stories like this (but with different endings) are seen in almost every newspaper, I might doubt this . . . but I don't . . .

"When I was a freshman in college I acquired a boy friend, my first and most intense. And after certain moonlit nights in spring—he jilted me.

"I suffered it with pride and bitterness, and when I finally was sure the brush-off had been permanent, I decided it was best to make an end of things. I bought enough iodine to fill an eight-ounce glass, and poured it out, when a girl, my best friend, from upstairs, came down.

"We had been discovering Brooke together, and she was giggling over the 'Chilterns':

> Your eyes, my dear adorable,
> Oh, I've loved you faithfully and well,
> Three years, or a bit less.
> It wasn't a success.

"I listened while she read it to me twice, and then I giggled too, and went in and poured my glass of iodine down the sink. It was as silly and as simple as all that, and Brooke has written many better poems, but that's the one I've memorized."

Because this girl now admits it was silly . . . let's pour her name down the sink too.

-»>«-

Here is a letter that speaks for itself . . . poems that influence decisions? . . .

"Yes, sure, I have one. Not a great poem. Not literature. Not even art, perhaps. But a poem that's known a damnsite better than a whole lot of fine art and that's quoted as much, almost, as the Bible: Kipling's 'On the Road to Mandalay.'

" 'Somewhere's East of Suez where the best is like the worst.' A heap of people know that better than they know their catechism.

" 'And there ain't no Ten Commandments and a man can raise a thirst.' I was young when those lines had their appeal. Young in a blasted Mid-West small town where the most exciting thing that ever happened was some farmer's cow having a new calf. A youth in a state of prairie vastness, yet shackled, like in a jail, with the Bible Belt conventions heavy around my feet.

By the old Moulmein pagoda, lookin' lazy at the sea.

Where the flyin' fishes play.

I seed her a'smokin' of a whackin' white cheroot

Where the dawn comes up like thunder outa China 'cross the bay.

Bloomin' idol made o' mud, what they calls the great god Budd.

"Those lines were not just jingles; they were pictures; they were romance, glamour, freedom, Life!

"I had to go and see those pictures. I had to sit by the old Moulmein pagoda and look lazy at the sea; I had to see the dawn like thunder, to hear the paddles chunkin', see the elephants a'pilin' teak. Oh, God, how my Mid-West tank town strangled me! I had to go and see those things, those places where people loved and fought and died—or I would have died smack in the middle of a million acres of corn.

"And the day came when I shook the dust of the Middle West from off my feet and let it be anathema— which was right as the Good Book said that they shoved so righteously down my throat.

"And, yes, I've sat by the old Moulmein pagoda and I've devoutly bought gold leaf and rubbed it on the golden face of the Great God Budd, and I've worked with the elephants a'pilin' teak, and I have *not* seen the dawn come up like thunder acrost the bay, 'cause at Moulmein there ain't no bay!

"And how did it affect my life?

"Thus: I'm listed in 'Who's Who' as an Oriental scholar and an explorer; and that first little escape from the eminently safe and sane small town home led on to the jungles of Africa and South America, and instead of being a prosperous grower of government subsidized wheat, I am a writer of abstruse geographical articles and books of travel and am as broke as any other pseudo-scholar who dabbles in things that interest nobody else.

"And the best thing I ever did in my most satisfactorily mis-spent life was to listen to the lilt of those verses and get out of my Mid-West prison to go look-see the pictures that a great man's poems conjured up.

Gordon MacCraegh."

9. DRESS PARADE

Dress Parade

→→»«←←

ALL of life is a reviewing stand and every day,
"Dress Parade." But behind the buttons and
braid are the hours of planning and toiling that
keep us in step in the line. Behind that is the dream,
the "Sim-Sali-Bim" of magic, the hocus-pocus of the
heart, the songs of the language called "poetry," the
favorite poems of all the people! The list is endless, so
obviously these pages can include only those representative poems which seem to have impressed the most people
or certain unusual poems cherished by the few.

Here are the favorites of eminently successful people
in all walks of life, the magic formulas that have secretly
influenced their decisions, the guiding philosophies on
which their successes have been built.

LOOK TO THIS DAY

Look to this day!
For it is Life, the very Life of Life.
In its brief course lie all the verities
And realities of your existence:
The bliss of growth,
The glory of action,
The splendor of beauty.

For yesterday is already a dream,
And tomorrow is only a vision;
But today, well-lived, makes every
Yesterday a dream of happiness,
And every tomorrow a vision of hope.

Look well therefore to this day!
Such is the salutation of the dawn.
                                    —Sanskrit.

PIPPA'S SONG

The year's at the spring
And day's at the morn;
Morning's at seven;
The hillside's dew-pearled;
The lark's on the wing;
The snail's on the thorn;
God's in his heaven—
All's right with the world.

—Robert Browning.

RUBAIYAT OF OMAR KHAYYAM

Wake! For the Sun who scattered into flight
The Stars before him from the Field of Night,
    Drives Night along with them from Heaven,
        and strikes
The Sultan's Turret with a Shaft of Light.

Before the phantom of False morning died,
Methought a Voice within the Tavern cried,
    "When all the Temple is prepared within,
Why nods the drowsy Worshipper outside?"

.   .   .   .

Come, fill the Cup, and in the fire of Spring
Your Winter-garment of Repentance fling:
    The Bird of Time has but a little way
To flutter—and the Bird is on the Wing.

Whether at Naishapur or Babylon,
Whether the Cup with sweet or bitter run,
    The Wine of Life keeps oozing drop by drop,
The Leaves of Life keep falling one by one.

.   .   .   .

A Book of Verses underneath the Bough,
A Jug of Wine, a Loaf of Bread—and Thou
    Beside me singing in the Wilderness—
Oh, Wilderness were Paradise enow!

Some for the Glories of this World; and some
Sigh for the Prophet's Paradise to come;
    Ah, take the Cash, and let the Credit go,
Nor heed the rumble of a distant Drum!

Look to the blowing Rose about us—"Lo,
Laughing," she says, "into the world I blow,
    At once the silken tassel of my Purse
Tear, and its Treasure on the Garden throw."

And those who husbanded the Golden grain,
And those who flung it to the winds like Rain,
    Alike to no such aureate Earth are turned
As, buried once, Men want dug up again.

The worldly Hope men set their Hearts upon
Turns Ashes—or it prospers; and anon,
    Like Snow upon the Desert's dusty Face,
Lighting a little hour or two—was gone.

.   .   .   .

Think, in this battered Caravanserai
Whose Portals are alternate Night and Day,
    How Sultan after Sultan with his Pomp
Abode his destined Hour, and went his way.

They say the Lion and the Lizard keep
The Courts where Jamshyd gloried and drank deep:
    And Bahram, that great Hunter—the Wild Ass
Stamps o'er his Head, but cannot break his Sleep.

I sometimes think that never blows so red
The Rose as where some buried Caesar bled;
    That every Hyacinth the Garden wears
Dropped in her Lap from some once lovely Head.

And this reviving Herb whose tender Green
Fledges the River-Lip on which we lean—
　　Ah, lean upon it lightly! for who knows
From what once lovely Lip it springs unseen!

.　　　.　　　.　　　.

Ah, my Beloved, fill the Cup that clears
To-day of past Regret and future Fears:
　　To-morrow!—Why, To-morrow I may be
Myself with Yesterday's Seven thousand Years.

For some we loved, the loveliest and the best
That from his Vintage rolling Time hath pressed,
　　Have drunk their Cup a Round or Two before,
And one by one crept silently to rest.

And we that now make merry in the Room
They left, and Summer dresses in new bloom,
　　Ourselves must we beneath the Couch of Earth
Descend—ourselves to make a Couch—for whom?

Ah, make the most of what we yet may spend,
Before we too into the Dust descend;
　　Dust into Dust, and under Dust, to lie,
Sans Wine, sans Song, sans Singer, and—sans End!

.　　　.　　　.　　　.

Why, all the Saints and Sages who discussed
Of the two Worlds so wisely—they are thrust
　　Like foolish Prophets forth; their Words to Scorn
Are scattered, and their Mouths are stopped with Dust.

.　　　.　　　.　　　.

With them the seed of Wisdom did I sow,
And with mine own hand wrought to make it grow;
　　And this was all the Harvest that I reaped—
"I came like Water, and like Wind I go."

Into this Universe, and *Why* not Knowing
Nor *Whence*, like Water willy-nilly flowing;
   And out of it, as Wind along the Waste,
I know not *Whither*, willy-nilly blowing.

What, without asking, hither hurried *Whence?*
And, without asking, *Whither* hurried hence!
   Oh, many a Cup of this forbidden Wine
Must drown the memory of that insolence!

      .   .   .

A Hair perhaps divides the False and True;
Yes; and a single Alif were the clue—
   Could you but find it—to the Treasure-house,
And peradventure to The Master too;

Whose secret Presence, through Creation's veins
Running Quicksilver-like eludes your pains;
   Taking all shapes from Mah to Mahi; and
They change and perish all—but He remains;

A moment guessed—then back behind the Fold
Immersed of Darkness round the Drama Rolled
   Which, for the Pastime of Eternity,
He doth Himself contrive, enact, behold.

      .   .   .

I sent my Soul through the Invisible
Some letter of that After-life to spell;
   And by and by my Soul returned to me,
And answered, "I Myself am Heaven and Hell."

      .   .   .

The Ball no question makes of Ayes and Noes,
But Here or There, as strikes the Player, goes;
   And He that tossed you down into the Field,
He knows about it all—He knows—HE knows!

The Moving Finger writes; and, having writ,
Moves on: nor all your Piety nor Wit
   Shall lure it back to cancel half a Line
Nor all your Tears wash out a Word of it.

    .   .   .   .

Yet Ah, that Spring should vanish with the Rose!
That Youth's sweet-scented manuscript should close!
   The Nightingale that in the branches sang,
Ah whence, and whither flown again, who knows!

Would but the Desert of the Fountain yield
One glimpse—if dimly, yet indeed, revealed,
   To which the fainting Traveller might spring,
As springs the trampled herbage of the field!

Would but some winged Angel ere too late
Arrest the yet unfolded Roll of Fate,
   And make the stern Recorder otherwise
Enregister, or quite obliterate!

Ah Love! could you and I with Him conspire
To grasp this sorry Scheme of Things entire,
   Would not we shatter it to bits—and then
Remould it nearer to the Heart's desire!

    .   .   .   .

Yon rising Moon that looks for us again—
How oft hereafter will she wax and wane;
   How oft hereafter rising look for us
Through this same Garden—and for one in vain!

And when like her, oh Saki, you shall pass
Among the Guests Star-scattered on the Grass,
   And in your joyous errand reach the spot
Where I made One—turn down an empty Glass!
                  —Edward Fitzgerald.

MIRACLES

Why, who makes much of a miracle?
As to me I know of nothing else but miracles,
Whether I walk the streets of Manhattan,
Or dart my sight over the roofs of houses toward the sky,
Or wade with naked feet along the beach just in the edge
    of the water,
Or stand under trees in the woods,
Or talk by day with any one I love,
Or sit at table at dinner with the rest,
Or look at strangers opposite me riding in the car.
Or watch honey-bees busy around the hive of a summer
    forenoon,
Or animals feeding in the fields,
Or birds, or the wonderfulness of insects in the air,
Or the wonderfulness of the sundown, or of stars shining
    so quiet and bright
Or the exquisite delicate thin curve of the new moon in
    spring;
These with the rest, one and all, are to me miracles,
The whole referring, yet each distinct and in its place.

To me every hour of the light and dark is a miracle,
Every cubic inch of space is a miracle,
Every square yard of the surface of the earth is spread
    with the same,
Every foot of the interior swarms with the same.

To me the sea is a continual miracle,
The fishes that swim—the rocks—the motion of the
    waves—
    the ships with men in them,
What stranger miracles are there?

                           —Walt Whitman.

All the world's a stage,
And all the men and women merely players:
They have their exits and their entrances;
And one man in his time plays many parts,
His acts being seven ages. At first the infant,
Mewling and puking in the nurse's arms.
And then the whining school-boy, with his satchel,
And shining morning face, creeping like snail
Unwillingly to school. And then the lover,
Sighing like furnace, with a woful ballad
Made to his mistress' eyebrow. Then a soldier,
Full of strange oaths, and bearded like the pard,
Jealous in honour, sudden and quick in quarrel,
Seeking the bubble reputation
Even in the cannon's mouth. And then the justice,
In fair round belly with good capon lin'd,
With eyes severe, and beard of formal cut,
Full of wise saws and modern instances;
And so he plays his part. The sixth age shifts
Into the lean and slipper'd pantaloon,
With spectacles on nose and pouch on side,
His youthful hose, well sav'd, a world too wide
For his shrunk shank; and his big manly voice,
Turning again toward childish treble, pipes
And whistles in his sound. Last scene of all,
That ends this strange eventful history,
Is second childishness and mere oblivion,
Sans teeth, sans eyes, sans taste, sans everything.
—William Shakespeare.*

A MAN'S PETITION

Let me live, O Mighty Master,
    Such a life as men should know,
Tasting triumph and disaster,
    Joy—and not too much of woe;

* *As You Like It*, Act II, Scene VII.

Let me run the gamut over,
    Let me fight and love and laugh
And when I'm beneath the clover
    Let this be my epitaph.

Here lies one who took his chances
    In life's busy world of men;
Battled fate and circumstances,
    Fought and fell and fought again.
Won sometimes, but did no crowing,
    Lost sometimes, but didn't wail,
Took his beating, but kept going
    Never let his courage fail.

He was fallible and human
    Therefore loved and understood
Both his fellow man and woman
    Whether good or not so good.
Kept his spirit undiminished,
    Never failed to help a friend,
Played the game till it was finished,
    Lived a Sportsman to the end.

                              —Unknown.

THE RHODORA:
ON BEING ASKED, WHENCE IS THE FLOWER?

In May, when sea-winds pierced our solitudes,
I found the fresh Rhodora in the woods,
Spreading its leafless blooms in a damp nook,
To please the desert and the sluggish brook.
The purple petals, fallen in the pool,
    Made the black water with their beauty gay;
Here might the red-bird come his plumes to cool,
    And court the flower that cheapens his array.
Rhodora! if the sages ask thee why
This charm is wasted on the earth and sky,

Tell them, dear, that if eyes were made for seeing,
Then Beauty is its own excuse for being:
   Why thou wert there, O rival of the rose!
I never thought to ask, I never knew:
   But, in my simple ignorance, suppose
The self-same power that brought me there brought you.
              —Ralph Waldo Emerson.

GOD MAKE ME WORTHY OF MY FRIENDS

It is my joy in life to find
   At every turning of the road
The strong arm of a comrade kind
   To help me onward with my load;
And since I have no gold to give
   'Tis love alone must make amends,
My only prayer is while I live—
   God make me worthy of my friends.
              —Unknown.

THE CHAMBERED NAUTILUS

This is the ship of pearl, which, poets feign,
   Sails the unshadowed main,—
   The venturous bark that flings
On the sweet summer wind its purpled wings
In gulfs enchanted, where the Siren sings,
   And coral reefs lie bare,
Where the cold sea-maids rise to sun their streaming hair.

Its webs of living gauze no more unfurl;
   Wrecked is the ship of pearl!
   And every chambered cell,
Where its dim dreaming life was wont to dwell,
As the frail tenant shaped his growing shell,
   Before thee lies revealed,—
Its irised ceiling rent, its sunless crypt unsealed!

Year after year beheld the silent toil
   That spread his lustrous coil;

Still, as the spiral grew,
He left the past year's dwelling for the new,
Stole with soft step its shining archway through,
    Built up its idle door,
Stretched in his last-found home, and knew the old no
    more.

Thanks for the heavenly message brought by thee,
    Child of the wandering sea,
    Cast from her lap, forlorn.
From thy dead lips a clearer note is born
Than ever Triton blew from his wreathed horn!
    While on mine ear it rings,
Through the deep caves of thought I hear a voice that
    sings—

Build thee more stately mansions, O my soul,
    As the swift seasons roll!
    Leave thy low-vaulted past!
Let each new temple, nobler than the last,
Shut thee from heaven with a dome more vast,
    Till thou at length art free,
Leaving thine outgrown shell by life's unresting sea!
                    —Oliver Wendell Holmes.

HAIL AND FAREWELL

An anxious generation sends you forth
On the far conquest of the Thrones of Might.
From East and West, from South and North,
Earth's children, weary-eyed by too much light,
Cry from their dream-forsaken vales of pain:
"Give us our gods! Give us our gods again!"
An hungry and relentless century, gazing with Argus-eye,
Has pierced the very inmost halls of Faith—
And left no shelter whither man may flee
From the cold storms of night and lovelessness and death.

Old gods have fallen. And the new must rise
Out of the dust of doubts and broken creeds;
The sons of those who cast mens' idols low
Must build up for a hungry people's needs
New gods, new hope, new strength to toil and grow . . .
The Portals are open. The wide road leads
Through thicket and garden, o'er stone and sod . . .
On! Up! Boots and saddles! Give spurs to your steeds!
There's a city beleaguered that cries for mens' deeds,
For the faith that is strength and the love that is God.
On through the dawning! Humanity calls!
Life's not a dream in the clover,—
On to the walls! On to the walls! On to the walls and over!
                                        —Hermann Hagedorn.

CROSSING THE BAR

Sunset and evening star,
    And one clear call for me!
And may there be no moaning of the bar,
    When I put out to sea,

But such a tide as moving seems asleep,
    Too full for sound and foam,
When that which drew from out the boundless deep
    Turns again home.

Twilight and evening bell,
    And after that the dark!
And may there be no sadness of farewell,
    When I embark;

For tho' from out our bourne of Time and Place
    The flood may bear me far,
I hope to see my Pilot face to face.
    When I have crossed the bar.
                                        —Alfred, Lord Tennyson.

LIFE'S SYMPHONY

"O Master, I would play the violin!
Pray try me! I am really not unskilled!"
The master with a patient gesture stilled
The ardent voice. "The music must begin—
Seest thou for violins I have no need.
Back to the wood-winds; take thine own bassoon
And play thy part." The strings were all in tune,
The brasses ready. Still the voice did plead
"O Master, I play only three short bars!"
"Thou playest the bassoon well—no more entreat—
Thy three short bars are needed to complete
The music that shall lift men to the stars!"

O Soul, play well the few notes given thee—
The Master needs them for Life's Symphony.
                              —B. Y. Williams.

SIMPLE SERVICE

If I can stop one heart from breaking
    I shall not live in vain;
If I can ease one life the aching
    Or cool one pain,
Or help one fainting robin
    Into its nest again,
I shall not live in vain.

                              —Unknown.

CARES

The little cares that fretted me,
    I lost them yesterday
Among the fields above the sea,
    Among the winds at play;

Among the lowing of the herds,
  The rustling of the trees,
Among the singing of the birds,
  The humming of the bees.

The foolish fears of what may happen,
  I cast them all away
Among the clover-scented grass,
  Among the new-mown hay;
Among the husking of the corn
  Where drowsy poppies nod,
Where ill thoughts die and good are born,
  Out in the fields with God.
                    —Elizabeth Barrett Browning.

INVICTUS

Out of the night that covers me,
  Black as the Pit from pole to pole,
I thank whatever gods may be
  For my unconquerable soul.

In the fell clutch of circumstance
  I have not winced nor cried aloud.
Under the bludgeonings of chance
  My head is bloody, but unbowed.

Beyond this place of wrath and tears
  Looms but the Horror of the shade,
And yet the menace of the years
  Finds, and shall find, me unafraid.

It matters not how strait the gate,
  How charged with punishments the scroll,
I am the master of my fate;
  I am the captain of my soul.
                    —William Ernest Henley.

POLONIUS'S ADVICE TO LAERTES

Give thy thoughts no tongue,
Nor any unproportion'd thought his act.
Be thou familiar, but by no means vulgar;
The friends thou hast, and their adoption tried,
Grapple them to thy soul with hoops of steel;
But do not dull thy palm with entertainment
Of each new-hatch'd unfledg'd comrade. Beware
Of entrance to a quarrel, but, being in,
Bear 't that th' opposed may beware of thee.
Give every man thine ear, but few thy voice;
Take each man's censure, but reserve thy judgment.
Costly thy habit as thy purse can buy,
But not express'd in fancy; rich, not gaudy;
For the apparel oft proclaims the man.

. . . .

Neither a borrower, nor a lender be;
For loan oft loses both itself and friend,
And borrowing dulls the edge of husbandry.
This above all: to thine own self be true,
And it must follow, as the night the day,
Thou canst not then be false to any man.
—William Shakespeare.*

THE LAST PRAYER OF SOCRATES

Beloved Pan, or any other gods who haunt this place,
Grant me an inner beauty of the soul.
May my inner and my outer man be as one,
May I count the wise only as wealthy
And have as much gold as a modest man can
carry with him.
—Unknown.

* *Hamlet*, Act I, Scene III.

SONNETS FROM THE PORTUGUESE

14.

If thou must love me, let it be for nought
Except for love's sake only. Do not say,
"I love her for her smile—her look—her way
Of speaking gently,—for a trick of thought
That falls in well with mine, and certes brought
A sense of pleasant ease on such a day;"—
For these things in themselves, beloved, may
Be changed, or change for thee,—and love so wrought
May be unwrought so. Neither love me for
Thine own dear pity's wiping my cheeks dry:
A creature might forget to weep, who bore
Thy comfort long, and lose thy love thereby.
But love me for love's sake, that evermore
Thou may'st love on through love's eternity.

43.

How do I love thee? Let me count the ways.
I love thee to the depth and breadth and height
My soul can reach, when feeling out of sight
For the ends of Being and ideal Grace.
I love thee to the level of everyday's
Most quiet need, by sun and candle-light.
I love thee freely, as men strive for Right;
I love thee purely, as men turn from Praise.
I love thee with the passion put to use
In my old griefs, and with my childhood's faith.
I love thee with a love I seemed to lose
With my lost saints,—I love thee with the breath,
Smiles, tears, of all my life!—and, if God choose,
I shall but love thee better after death.
                    —Elizabeth Barrett Browning.

BUILDING THE BRIDGE FOR HIM

An old man, traveling a lone highway,
Came at the evening cold and gray,
To a chasm deep and wide.

The old man crossed in the twilight dim,
For the sullen stream held no fears for him.
But he turned when he reached the other side
And builded a bridge to span the tide.

"Old man," cried a fellow pilgrim near,
"You are wasting your strength with building here;
Your journey will end with the ending day,
And you never again will pass this way.

"You have crossed the chasm deep and wide.
Why build you a bridge at eventide?"
And the builder raised his old gray head:
"Good friend, on the path I have come," he said,
"There followeth after me today
A youth whose feet will pass this way.

"This stream, which has been as naught to me
To that fair-haired boy may a pitfall be;
He, too, must cross in the twilight dim—
Good friend, I am building this bridge for him."
                              —W. A. Dromgoole.

ABOU BEN ADHEM

Abou Ben Adhem (may his tribe increase!)
Awoke one night from a deep dream of peace,
And saw, within the moonlight in his room,
Making it rich, and like a lily in bloom,
An angel writing in a book of gold:—
Exceeding peace had made Ben Adhem bold,
And to the presence in the room he said,

"What writest thou?"—The vision raised its head,
And with a look made of all sweet accord,
Answered, "The names of those who love the Lord."
"And is mine one?" said Abou. "Nay, not so,"
Replied the angel. Abou spoke more low,
But cheerily still; and said, "I pray thee, then,
Write me as one that loves his fellow-men."

The Angel wrote, and vanished. The next night
It came again with a great wakening light,
And showed the names whom love of God had blessed,
And, lo! Ben Adhem's name led all the rest.
—Leigh Hunt.

THE MARSHES OF GLYNN

. . . .

Ye marshes, how candid and simple and nothing-with-
    holding and free
Ye publish yourselves to the sky and offer yourselves to
    the sea!
Tolerant plains, that suffer the sea and the rains and
    the sun,
Ye spread and span like the catholic man who hath
    mightily won
God out of knowledge and good out of infinite pain
And sight out of blindness and purity out of a stain.

As the marsh-hen secretly builds on the watery sod,
Behold I will build me a nest on the greatness of God:
I will fly in the greatness of God as the marsh-hen flies
In the freedom that fills all the space 'twixt the marsh and
    the skies:
By so many roots as the marsh-grass sends in the sod
I will heartily lay me a-hold on the greatness of God:
Oh, like to the greatness of God is the greatness within
The range of the marshes, the liberal marshes of Glynn.

And the sea lends large. as the marsh: lo, out of his plenty
   the sea
Pours fast: full soon the time of the flood tide must be:
Look how the grace of the sea doth go
About and about through the intricate channels that flow
                  Here and there,
                  Everywhere,
Till his waters have flooded the uttermost creeks and the
   low-lying lanes,
And the marsh is meshed with a million veins,
That like as with rosy and silvery essences flow
In the rose-and-silver evening glow.
                Farewell, my lord Sun!
The creeks overflow: a thousand rivulets run
'Twixt the roots of the sod; the blades of the marsh grass
   stir;
Passeth a hurrying sound of wings that westward whirr;
Passeth, and all is still; and the currents cease to run;
And the sea and the marsh are one.

How still the plains of the waters be!
The tide is in his ecstasy;
The tide is at his highest height:
              And it is night.
And now from the Vast of the Lord will the waters of
   sleep
Roll in the souls of men,
But who will reveal to our waking ken
The forms that swim and the shapes that creep
           Under the waters of sleep?
And I would I could know what swimmeth below when
   the tide comes in
On the length and the breadth of the marvelous marshes
   of Glynn.
                —Sidney Lanier.

HOME-THOUGHTS, FROM ABROAD

Oh, to be in England
Now that April's there,
And whoever wakes in England
Sees, some morning, unaware,
That the lowest boughs and the brushwood sheaf
Round the elm-tree bole are in tiny leaf,
While the chaffinch sings on the orchard bough
In England—now!

And after April, when May follows,
And the whitethroat builds, and all the swallows!
Hark, where my blossomed pear-tree in the hedge
Leans to the field and scatters on the clover
Blossoms and dewdrops—at the bent spray's edge—
That's the wise thrush; he sings each song twice over,
Lest you should think he never could recapture
The first fine careless rapture!
And though the fields look rough with hoary dew
All will be gay when noontide wakes anew
The buttercups, the little children's dower
—Far brighter than this gaudy melon-flower!

—Robert Browning.

ELEGY WRITTEN IN A COUNTRY
CHURCHYARD

The curfew tolls the knell of parting day,
    The lowing herd winds slowly o'er the lea,
The plowman homeward plods his weary way,
    And leaves the world to darkness and to me.

.   .   .   .   .

Beneath those rugged elms, that yew-tree's shade,
    Where heaves the turf in many a mouldering heap,
Each in his narrow cell for ever laid,
    The rude forefathers of the hamlet sleep.

.   .   .   .   .

For them no more the blazing hearth shall burn,
   Or busy housewife ply her evening care:
No children run to lisp their sire's return,
   Or climb his knees the envied kiss to share.

Oft did the harvest to their sickle yield,
   Their furrow oft the stubborn glebe has broke:
How jocund did they drive their team afield!
   How bowed the woods beneath their sturdy stroke!

Let not Ambition mock their useful toil,
   Their homely joys, and destiny obscure;
Nor Grandeur hear with a disdainful smile
   The short and simple annals of the poor.

The boast of heraldry, the pomp of power
   And all that beauty, all that wealth e'er gave.
Await alike the inevitable hour:
   The paths of glory lead but to the grave.

Nor you, ye proud, impute to these the fault
   If Memory o'er their tomb no trophies raise,
Where through the long-drawn aisle and fretted vault
   The pealing anthem swells the note of praise.

Can storied urn or animated bust
   Back to its mansion call the fleeting breath?
Can Honour's voice provoke the silent dust,
   Or Flattery soothe the dull cold ear of death?

Perhaps in this neglected spot is laid
   Some heart once pregnant with celestial fire;
Hands, that the rod of empire might have swayed,
   Or waked to ecstasy the living lyre.

Full many a gem of purest ray serene
   The dark unfathomed caves of ocean bear:
Full many a flower is born to blush unseen,
   And waste its sweetness on the desert air.

Some village Hampden that, with dauntless breast,
   The little tyrant of his fields withstood,
Some mute inglorious Milton here may rest,
   Some Cromwell guiltless of his country's blood.

.   .   .   .

Far from the madding crowd's ignoble strife,
   Their sober wishes never learned to stray;
Along the cool, sequestered vale of life
   They kept the noiseless tenor of their way.

Yet even these bones from insult to protect
   Some frail memorial still erected nigh,
With uncouth rhymes and shapeless sculpture decked,
   Implores the passing tribute of a sigh.

THE EPITAPH

Here rests his head upon the lap of Earth
   A youth, to fortune and to fame unknown.
Fair Science frowned not on his humble birth,
   And Melancholy marked him for her own.

Large was his bounty, and his soul sincere,
   Heaven did a recompense as largely send:
He gave to Misery (all he had) a tear,
   He gained from Heaven ('twas all he wished) a friend.

No farther seek his merits to disclose,
   Or draw his frailties from their dread abode,
(There they alike in trembling hope repose,)
   The bosom of his Father and his God.
                —Thomas Gray.

PIONEERS! O PIONEERS!

Come, my tan-faced children,
Follow well in order, get your weapons ready,
Have you your pistols? have you your sharp-edged axes?
    Pioneers! O pioneers!

For we cannot tarry here,
We must march my darlings, we must bear the brunt of
        danger,
We the youthful sinewy races, all the rest on us depend,
    Pioneers! O pioneers!

O you youths, Western youths,
So impatient, full of action, full of manly pride and
        friendship
Plain I see you Western youths, see you tramping with
        the foremost,
    Pioneers! O pioneers!

Have the elder races halted.
Do they droop and end their lesson, wearied over there
        beyond the seas?
We take up the task eternal, and the burden and the
        lesson,
    Pioneers! O pioneers!

From Nebraska, from Arkansas,
Central inland race are we, from Missouri, with the
        continental blood intervein'd,
All the hands of comrades clasping, all the Southern, all
        the Northern,
    Pioneers! O pioneers!

O resistless restless race!
O beloved race in all! O my breast aches with tender love
        for all!
O I mourn and yet exult, I am rapt with love for all,
    Pioneers! O pioneers!

On and on the compact ranks,
With accessions ever waiting, with the places of the dead
    quickly fill'd,
Through the battle, through defeat, moving yet and
    never stopping,
  Pioneers! O pioneers!

O to die advancing on!
Are there some of us to droop and die? has the hour
    come?
Then upon the march we fittest die, soon and sure the
    gap is fill'd,
  Pioneers! O pioneers!

Do the feasters gluttonous feast?
Do the corpulent sleepers sleep? Have they lock'd and
    bolted doors?
Still be ours the diet hard, and the blanket on the ground,
  Pioneers! O pioneers!

Has the night descended?
Was the road of late so toilsome? did we stop dis-
    couraged nodding on our way?
Yet a passing hour I yield you in your tracks to pause
    oblivious,
  Pioneers! O pioneers!

Till with sound of trumpet,
Far, far off the daybreak call—hark! how loud and clear I
    hear it wind,
Swift! to the head of the army!—swift! spring to your
    places,
  Pioneers! O pioneers!
                                    —Walt Whitman.

MIZPAH

Go thou thy way, and I go mine,
  Apart, yet not afar;
Only a thin veil hangs between
  The pathways where we are.
And "God keep watch 'tween thee and me" . . .
  This is my prayer.
He looks thy way, He looketh mine,
  And keeps us near.

I know not where thy road may lie,
  Or which way mine will be;
If mine will lead through parching sands,
  And thine beside the sea;
Yet God keeps watch 'tween thee and me;
  So never fear.
He holds thy hand, He claspeth mine,
  And keeps us near.

Should wealth and fame perchance be thine,
  And my lot lowly be;
Or you be sad and sorrowful
  And glory be for me,
Yet God keep watch 'tween thee and me,
  Both be His care.
One arm 'round thee and one 'round me
  Will keep us near . . .

And though our paths be separate,
  And thy way is not mine,
Yet, coming to the mercy-seat,
  My soul will meet with thine,
And "God keep watch 'tween thee and me,"
  I'll whisper there.
He blesseth thee, He blesseth me,
  And we are near.

                              —Julia Baker.

A PSALM OF LIFE

Tell me not, in mournful numbers,
  Life is but an empty dream!—
For the soul is dead that slumbers,
  And things are not what they seem.

Life is real! Life is earnest!
  And the grave is not its goal;
Dust thou art, to dust returnest,
  Was not spoken of the soul.

    .   .   .   .

Art is long, and Time is fleeting,
  And our hearts, though stout and brave,
Still, like muffled drums, are beating
  Funeral marches to the grave.

In the world's broad field of battle,
  In the bivouac of Life,
Be not like dumb, driven cattle!
  Be a hero in the strife!

Trust no Future, howe'er pleasant!
  Let the dead Past bury its dead!
Act,—act in the living Present!
  Heart within, and God o'erhead!

Lives of great men all remind us
  We can make our lives sublime,
And, departing, leave behind us
  Footprints on the sands of time;

Footprints, that perhaps another,
  Sailing o'er life's solemn main,
A forlorn and shipwrecked brother,
  Seeing, shall take heart again.

Let us, then, be up and doing,
　　With a heart for any fate;
Still achieving, still pursuing,
　　Learn to labor and to wait.
　　　　　　　—Henry Wadsworth Longfellow.

TWENTY-THIRD PSALM

The Lord is my shepherd;
I shall not want.

He maketh me to lie down in green pastures:
He leadeth me beside the still waters.

He restoreth my soul:
He leadeth me in the paths of righteousness for His
　name's sake.

Yea, though I walk through the valley
Of the shadow of death, I will fear no evil:
For Thou art with me:
Thy rod and Thy staff they comfort me.

Thou preparest a table before me
In the presence of mine enemies:
Thou anointest my head with oil;
My cup runneth over.

Surely goodness and mercy
Shall follow me all the days of my life,
And I will dwell in the house of the Lord forever.
　　　　　　　—The Bible.

WAITING

Serene, I fold my hands and wait,
　　Nor care for wind, or tide, or sea;
I rave no more 'gainst Time or Fate,
　　For, lo! my own shall come to me.

I stay my haste, I make delays,
   For what avails this eager pace?—
I stand amid the eternal ways,
   And what is mine shall know my face.

Asleep, awake, by night or day,
   The friends I seek are seeking me;
No wind can drive my bark astray,
   Nor change the tide of destiny.

What matter if I stand alone?
   I wait with joy the coming years;
My heart shall reap what it hath sown,
   And garner up its fruits of tears.

The waters know their own and draw
   The brook that springs in yonder heights;
So flows the good with equal law
   Unto the soil of pure delights.

The stars come nightly to the sky;
   The tidal wave comes to the sea;
Nor time, nor pace, nor deep, nor high,
   Can keep my own away from me.
               —John Burroughs.

THANATOPSIS

So live, that when thy summons comes to join
That innumerable caravan, which moves
To that mysterious realm, where each shall take
His chamber in the silent halls of death,
Thou go not, like the quarry-slave at night,
Scourged to his dungeon, but, sustained and soothed
By an unfaltering trust, approach thy grave
Like one who wraps the drapery of his couch
About him, and lies down to pleasant dreams.
               —William Cullen Bryant.

THE DAY IS DONE

The day is done, and the darkness
   Falls from the wings of Night,
As a feather is wafted downward
   From an eagle in his flight.

I see the lights of the village
   Gleam through the rain and the mist,
And a feeling of sadness comes o'er me
   That my soul cannot resist:

A feeling of sadness and longing,
   That is not akin to pain,
And resembles sorrow only
   As the mist resembles the rain.

Come, read to me some poem,
   Some simple and heartfelt lay,
That shall soothe this restless feeling,
   And banish the thoughts of day.

Not from the grand old masters,
   Not from the bards sublime,
Whose distant footsteps echo
   Through the corridors of Time.

For, like strains of martial music,
   Their mighty thoughts suggest
Life's endless toil and endeavor;
   And to-night I long for rest.

Read from some humbler poet,
   Whose songs gushed from his heart,
As showers from the clouds of summer,
   Or tears from the eyelids start;

Who, through long days of labor,
And nights devoid of ease,
Still heard in his soul the music
Of wonderful melodies.

Such songs have power to quiet
The restless pulse of care,
And come like the benediction
That follows after prayer.

Then read from the treasured volume
The poem of thy choice,
And lend to the rhyme of the poet
The beauty of thy voice.

And the night shall be filled with music,
And the cares, that infest the day,
Shall fold their tents, like the Arabs,
And as silently steal away.
                    —Henry Wadsworth Longfellow.

BOASTS IN TOASTS

Drink to fair woman, who, I think,
Is most entitled to it,
For if anything can ever drive me to drink,
She certainly could do it.
                    —Unknown.

->>><<<-

Here's to the lasses we've loved, my lad,
Here's to the lips we've pressed;
For of kisses and lasses,
Like liquor in glasses,
The last is always the best.
                    —Unknown.

≫≪

If on my theme I rightly think,
There are five reasons why I drink:
Good wine, a friend, because I'm dry,
Or lest I should be by and by.
Or any other reason why.

—Dean Henry Aldrich.

≫≪

"Go ask papa," the maiden said,
But the young man knew her papa was dead,
And he knew the life her papa had led,
So she knew that he knew what she meant when she said,
"Go ask papa."

—Unknown.

≫≪

He is not drunk who, from the floor,
Can rise again and drink some more;
But he is drunk, who prostrate lies,
And cannot drink or cannot rise.

—Unknown.

≫≪

Here is a riddle most abstruse:
Canst read the answer right?
Why is it that my tongue grows loose
Only when I am tight?

—Unknown.

≫≪

Here's to the girl who is mine—all mine.
She drinks and she bets, and she smokes cigarettes,
And sometimes, I am told, she goes out and forgets
—that she's mine—all mine!

—Unknown.

10. TATTOO

Tattoo

→»)«←

ANY list of favorite quotations of famous people necessarily would be endless. They are the stories on which we sharpen our swords for daily battle, the needle of the compass that always points in the direction we want to travel, the mystic words we utter as we rub the magic lamp. They are the phrases that persist when all else is forgotten, tattooed indelibly on the language of the race. Here are a few of these lines and scattered verses to remind you of the many more that play a daily part in the lives of interesting people and to suggest the infinite number available to share your adventure with you.

Joan Bennett's favorite quotation comes from Thomas Hood's "Bridge of Sighs." Tyrone Power chooses A. E. Housman's "Shropshire Lad." Linda Darnell, who reads Spanish poetry in the original, nevertheless turns to "Don't Quit," an inspirational poem included in another section. Sheldon Leonard, who plays gangster types in the movies, considers Vachel Lindsay's "Song of the Congo" the most moving of all modern poems.

→»)«←

When Stanley Armstrong Hunter, pastor of St. John's Presbyterian Church, Berkeley, California, was a student at Princeton University, he had as one of his classmates the now distinguished commentator, David Lawrence. Dr. Hunter still recalls a framed card or motto on Lawrence's desk:

Build a little fence of trust around today,
Fill in the space with loving words and therein stay,
Look not through the sheltering bars upon tomorrow,
God will help thee bear what comes of joy or sorrow.

→»×«←

From the big roll-top desk in his newspaper office on the Main Street of Emporia, Kansas, William Allen White wrote:

"I think if any single piece of literature has been my guide and beacon, it is Emerson's essay on 'Self-reliance,' and the sentence, 'Rely on your own self. Every heart vibrates to that iron string.'"

→»×«←

Congressman Phil A. Bennett of Missouri, had to think back a good many years to remember where he first heard the quotation that has most affected his life:

"When a struggling young editor of a county seat newspaper, I received as a gift from a relative a large and beautifully engraved copy of Ella Wheeler Wilcox's lines:

There is so much bad in the best of us
And so much good in the worst of us,
It scarcely behooves any of us
To say anything about the rest of us.

"I hung this gift in a conspicuous place in my room and still have it after thirty years. I know that its influence helped to make me tolerant of the other fellow's views and has tempered my statements on many occasions."

→»×«←

Reading the always interesting stories of Faith Baldwin, I used to wonder where her endless fount of energy and inspiration came from, and so one day I asked her.

"On my desk in a book I use every day is a quotation from Kahlil Gibran. It is not poetry in the sense of rhymed verse, but it is as near as I have come to a working creed. I read it every day. I believe in it. It is truer to me every hour I live. Nothing I have ever read has meant as much to me, in a certain sense. This is what it says:

"You often say, I would give only to the deserving. The trees in your orchard say not so, nor the flocks in your pasture. They give that they may live, for to withhold is to perish.'"

→≫≍≪←

One of the mystic, and at the same time magic, qualities of poetry is its capacity to hold volumes of meaning in the briefest sentences. For example, these quotations in a letter from Luigi Lucioni, well-known artist:

"It is hard to say just which poem has played a part in my life and career. I have two favorites and both for different reasons. One is a short poem called 'Richard Cory,' by E. A. Robinson, and the other is called 'With Esther,' by William S. Blunt. The line that touches me deeply in it is:

> He can bear to die
> He who has once been happy.

"The 'Richard Cory' played a very strong part in my student days—when I would feel particularly depressed and envious of great success, I always thought of Richard Cory, who:

> Went home and put a bullet through his head."

→≫≍≪←

From a busy desk in the Halls of Congress, Representative Carl T. Curtis of Nebraska wrote one day:

"There are two poems that I frequently quote because I like the philosophy of them. I do not know who wrote either of them. One is:

> When I meet a man,
>   That seems to have gone astray
> I love to think he started right,
>   But merely lost his way.

"The other poem that I use often is:

> Only men can make
>   A nation great and strong,
> Men who for truth and honor's sake
>   Stand fast and suffer long."

→»×«←

Mignon G. Eberhardt, the author, harks back to a quotation associated with a period of illness.

"I was struggling and needed the steadfast sturdiness of these words:

> Come into port nobly, or sail with God the seas.

"'There's pride in it and a whole-heartedness that for many years has made it pop into my mind at all kinds of times with a kind of command to say 'stiffen up the spine,' and whether it's doing or giving or living, to do it fully. I don't claim to have come into every port I sailed for nobly, but I do think the words have a beauty and a comfort and a strength."

→»×«←

The poems we quote . . . the arrows we shoot into the air . . . the songs we sing . . . Here is a poem Rev. Roy C. Helfensten, minister of Mason City, Iowa, has made an intregral part of his own life as he has shared it with others:

"Douglas Mallock's poem 'Hills Ahead' was a great help to me in an experience of a large undertaking when reverses and obstacles beset me at every hand.

The hills ahead look hard and steep and high
And often we behold them with a sigh;
But as we near them level grows the road.
We find on every slope with every load
The climb is not so steep, the top so far,
The hills ahead look harder than they are.

And so it is with troubles though they seem so great
That men complain and fear and hesitate;
Less difficult the journey than we dreamed
It never proves as hard as once it seemed,
There never comes a task, a hill, a day
But as we near it—easier the way.

"The poem gave me new courage for the tasks ahead and the joy of unique achievement was realized. Since then I have used the poem many times in interviews with discouraged folk, who have said that it gave them new hope and new confidence. It has been a daily help to me in all my work."

->>x<<-

One of the interesting things about quotations is that they keep "popping up." For years my dad has quoted four lines to me until I find myself using them occasionally. You can imagine my feelings on reading the following from Clarence J. Brown, Representative from Ohio:
"Do you remember the lines that go something like this?

Vice is a monster of so dreadful mien
As to be hated needs but to be seen.
Yet seen too oft, familiar with her face,
We first endure, then pity, then embrace.

"I learned that poem many years ago as a youngster. It has been valuable to me many times since, and perhaps would be worth a little something to many others just now."

→»«←

It's curious how a phrase will stick . . . when all else is forgotten . . . .

"Twenty-four years ago, I was reading a book which had the following verse at the beginning. I do not know the author or whether I quote it perfectly, but it was like this," wrote Rev. Arthur M. Clarke, minister of Boone, Iowa:

> There is a room wherein no one enters,
>   Save I, myself, alone.
> There sits a blessed Memory upon a throne;
>   There my life centers.

"The verse caught me at once. It made me realize how important were the memories I was storing up for the future. It made me resolve to furnish that memory room with beautiful pictures. I have not entirely succeeded, but the resolution has remained with me."

→»«←

June Hynd, diminutive NBC commentator, not only preaches, but practices, this gem from literature:

"Had I but two loaves of bread, I would sell one and buy white hyacinths to feed my soul."

→»«←

Dr. Louie D. Newton, Atlanta minister, suggests a philosophy of infinite faith in his favorite quotation:

> On a branch that swings
> Sits a bird that sings
> Knowing that he has wings.
>   —Victor Hugo.

→»«←

Dr. John Mantey, of the Northern Baptist Theological Seminary, has a good reason for remembering an Ella Wheeler Wilcox stanza.

"At the age of sixteen or seventeen, after reading part of the New Testament and being deeply moved by it, I decided to become a Christian, in spite of a very unfavorable home and community environment. The thing I feared most was that some of my companions would ridicule me and call me a 'sissy.'

"It was in that critical period of character formation that I read and memorized this poem:

> One ship goes east, another west
>   By the selfsame wind that blows.
> 'Tis the set of the sail, and not the goal
>   That decides the way each goes.
> Like the winds of the sea are the ways of fate
>   As we voyage along through life.
> 'Tis the set of the soul that decides the goal
>   And not the calm nor the strife."

Editor, author, and poet himself, Ludwig Lewisohn knows well the magic of lines that cling in memory.

"There are lines from a poem which have meant a good deal to me through the dark and the light, more especially the dark, and the lines are:

> But tasks in hours of insight willed,
> May be in hours of gloom fulfilled.

"The title is 'Morality,' and the author Matthew Arnold."

Representative Thomas A. Jenkins wrote of his favorite quotation:

"I live in southern Ohio on the Ohio River. We have great floods there occasionally. Once when we had a great flood with the town well under water, with all lights out and all gas turned off, with the cold winds blowing and the snow flurries scattering, someone began a poem I shall never forget:

> It may not be my way,
> It may not be thy way,
> But God in his own way,
> Will always provide."

>>>≫≪<<

From Hollywood, Douglas MacLean, the actor, tells the interesting story associated with a verse he has often used:

"When I was a very small lad my grandfather, Colonel George P. MacLean of Philadelphia, insisted that I memorize what he called 'The Gentleman's Code.' He told me I might find it difficult, at times, to be faithful to it. He assured me, however, it was a grand thing to be trying and a lifetime of endeavor should produce some measure of success and pleasant satisfaction. Anyway, I gave him my promise to try. Here it is:

> Think big. Talk small.
> Love much. Laugh easily.
> Work happily. Play fair.
> Pay cash, and be kind.

"He was right about it being a grand thing to try. It's sort of like a golf game; you may not be able to make all the holes in par, but if you make a few, and possibly a couple of birdies, it helps a lot to make the final score more satisfying."

>>>≫≪<<

Occupied as he is with the problems of government, Congressman William T. Pheiffer finds certain phrases that have persisted in his memory:

"While, I regret to say, the busy life I have led has precluded me from very close contact with the Muses, yet you may find the following Latin proverb, which has buoyed me up at critical times, of interest:

"'Per aspera ad astra.' (Through difficulties to the stars.)

"In lighter vein, my favorite epigram is:

The boy who stopped on third base to congratulate himself did not make the home run."

→»≫«←

It would be interesting to know where our favorite quotations first entered into our pattern of life, where we first read them or heard them, as Rev. T. G. Hartwig tells.

"There is a most truthful, as well as beautiful, little aphorism that my sainted mother dictated to my youthful mind, which reads as follows:

If Wisdom's ways you'd wisely seek,
    Five things observe with care—
Of whom you speak,—
To whom you speak,—
    And How, and When and Where.

"Throughout my ministry of over thirty-six years, I have carried the happy testimonial deep in my heart of hearts. Those treasured words have so oft steadied my restless soul, so prone to conflict with the cherished opinions of others."

→»≫«←

There seems to be no end to the services of poetry. . . .

"One poem that has given me three book titles is by Henry van Dyke and it starts out:

> Oh, London is a man's town
> There's power in the air—
> And Paris is a woman's town
> With flowers in her hair.

"'Paris is a Woman's Town' and 'London is a Man's Town' were the titles of two travel books I did some years ago with Helen Josephy, and now I'm at it again. My new book is 'America for Me.'
>   —Mary Margaret McBride."

>>*<<

Congressman Cleff Clevenger, from Ohio, quotes as his favorite line:

> Be noble, my son, and the nobleness that in other
>   men lies
> Sleeping but never dead, shall rise in majesty to
>   meet thine own.

>>*<<

From Ward Melville comes a story of the surprising results of a casual phrase.

"When I was fourteen or fifteen years old the Headmaster of my preparatory school spent a week-end at my home on the North Shore of Long Island. Just at sunset we were driving home along the east side of Setauket Harbor, when silhouetted against the red of the sunset were the spars of a cargo schooner which had been beached and abandoned some years before and left to rot away on the shore. The sight was striking and beautiful.

"My Headmaster quoted the following words:

> There is never a flood comes landward now,
>   But lifts a hulk we have manned;
> There is never an ebb goes seaward now,
>   But moves our dead on the sands.

"The words were unfamiliar and excited my interest. After dinner that night the Headmaster produced a small book of Kipling's poems and not only read the complete poem from which he had quoted, but several other similar pieces. From that time on I have been a lover of Kipling, of whom I had at that time not even heard, and I firmly believe that he has given me more pleasure in my life than any other one thing to which I can point."

->>><<-

This last quotation, from Mr. C. S. Anderson, Wisconsin industrialist, happens to be one of my favorites, too. I found it on the bottom of a convention program when I was about fourteen years old and it has inspired many a game for me ever since.

Mr. Anderson says:

"There hangs in my office, and has hung there for many years, a placard which bears the following motto:

> For when the one great scorer comes
> To write against your name,
> He writes—not that you won or lost,
> But how you played the game.

"This has always proved an inspiration and guide to me."

->>><<-

I suppose everyone has a favorite 'quotation.' I wonder what yours is!

11. TO QUARTERS

To Quarters

➻❯❮❰

EVENING

Let this house be journey's end;
   Here is rest to borrow;
Sleep hath only peace to lend
To the long day's labor, friend—
   Sleep until tomorrow!

Here's a hearthplace, here is food,
   Here there is no hurry
For the fretful and the rude
Workings of an old earth's mood—
   Let tomorrow worry!

For the day's long labor, friend,
   There'll be time tomorrow!
Let this house be journey's end,
Sleep hath only peace to lend—
   Come you in and borrow!
             —Bert Cooksley.

WANDERERS RETURN

Let me come to you as a friend would do
   After a lengthy journey; one who stands
With much of earth's warm sun and cooling dew,
   Articulate on her face, with far off lands
Signatured on her brain—and with desire
   To find beside your hearth her journey's end;

To bring within your home the precious fire
   That has the forthright, simple name, of Friend.
And let your ways and moods continue on
   Just as they've done; let me become a part
Of what you are; bring back nothing that's gone
   Hide nothing that remains, just let my heart
Be one with you and yours, and bit by bit
Learn all those truths for which God fashioned it.
                 —Frances Cansella.

RADIO

All afternoon wind and rain
   Swept the valley . . . But with the night
Came peace and a great golden moon
   Above the highest hill—full and bright.
Surely you remember . . . And then your voice
   Broke the stillness of dim space—O son of mine!
Within this little house your presence glowed once
    more;
   It was as though you stepped, in all your youth
   divine,
Through my open waiting door
And came to me . . . You sang the old, old song
   My mother sang long years ago,
The song I crooned to you within the valley dusk,
   With tall hills listening in a row;
O son of mine—each note, each dear, familiar word,
   Came ringing from across a distant sea
And traced themselves indelibly, through miles of night
   Upon the mother's heart of me . . .

Jim, your dog, came close and softly cried,
   Within his old dim eyes a wandering stare—
Then ran with eager labored step
   And brought your slippers to your chair.
                 —Dorothy Beedy.

LEAF BURNING

I swept the fallen leaves up yesterday
  And touched them with slow fire;
And as I saw smoke rise and drift away
  I knew a keen desire.

To sweep my mind of old things lying there,
  Dreams long since dead . . .
Hopes that have clung like leaves on boughs now bare,
  And tears that I have shed . . .

I longed to gather every little grief
  Left scattered round,
Small doubts and fears and lay them in a sheaf
  On fire, smoke crowned.

Then stir the embers so a laughing wind
  Might lift the ashes of old praise or blame
And bear them far away, leaving my mind
  Clean as if swept by flame.
                              —Virginia Eaton

REQUIEM

Under the wide and starry sky
Dig the grave and let me lie;
Glad did I live and gladly die,
  And I laid me down with a will.

This be the verse you 'grave for me:
Here he lies where he long'd to be;
Home is the sailor, home from the sea,
  And the hunter home from the hill.
                        —Robert Louis Stevenson.

GOD'S BONFIRES

I'm glad that God takes every worn-out day
　And burns it up in sunset; all mistakes,
The little triumphs and the futile cares
　Are fathered in to one bonfire that breaks
In flame against the banks of sky. I think
　That God sweeps up the grayed-out ends of day
And says: "Poor, foolish children—this the spoil
　Of all their goods. When will they learn the way
But since these things are done, we might as well
　Make one great conflagration of it all."
I think He likes to see it burn, and stands
　Beside it till the last gray ashes fall.

And then across the fretful thoroughfares,
　Over the troubled roofs and petty wars, .
Out of the lonely heights of the Unknown,
　A clean wind blows, all tangled up with stars.
　　　　　　　　　　　　—Velma Bell.

➤➤❯❮❮

BENEDICTION

The sun be warm and kind
　To you,
The darkest night, some star
　Shine through,
The dullest morn
　A radiance brew,
And when dusk comes—
God's hand
　To you.
　　　　　　　—Eleanor Powers McCann.

I AM WEARY OF BEING BITTER

I am weary of being bitter and weary of being wise,
 And the armor and the mask of these fall from me,
  after long.
I would go where the islands sleep, or where the sea-
  dawns rise,
 And lose my bitter wisdom in the wisdom of a song.

There are magics in melodies, unknown of the sages;
 The powers of purest wonder on secret wings go by.
Doubtless out of the silence of dumb preceding ages
 Song woke the chaos-world—and light swept the sky.

All that we know is idle; idle is all we cherish;
 Idle the will that takes loads that proclaim it strong.
For the knowledge, the strength, the burden—all
  shall perish;
 One thing only endures, one thing only—song.
      —Arthur Davison Ficke.

GIFTS WITHOUT SEASON

Lord, I would thank You for these things:
 Not sunlight only, but sullen rain;
Not only laughter with lifted wings,
 But the heavy muted hands of pain.

Lord, I would thank You for so much:
 The toil no less than the well-earned ease;
The glory always beyond our touch
 That bows the head and bends the knees.

Lord, there are gifts of brighter gold
 Than the deepest mine or mint can yield:
Friendship and love and a dream to hold,
 The look that heartened, the word that healed.

Lord, I would thank You for eyes to see
   Miracles in our everyday earth:
The colors that crowd monotony,
   The flame of the humblest flower's birth.

Lord, I would thank You for gifts without season:
   The flash of a thought like a banner unfurled,
The splendor of faith and the sparkle of reason,
   The tolerant mind in a turbulent world!
                    —Joseph Auslander.

HEART AT PEACE

The wounds of words are water in the wind,
   When time has blown the long slow hours by
And memory is something worn and thinned
   With secret handling. Then the old wounds lie
As lightly as the ripples on a lake;
   There is no word, however harsh, can touch
More than the surface of an old heartbreak,
   When dreams are dead and one has borne too much.

The wounds of words are wind among the leaves—
   Only a murmur somewhere over head,
A whisper that is heard but hardly grieves
   The heart that went too long uncomforted,
And rose, resolved to play no more the lover—
The heart at peace that lets all wounds blow over.
                  —Helen Frazee-Bower.

TEARS

When I consider Life and its few years—
   A wisp of fog betwixt us and the sun;
   A call to battle, and the battle done
Ere the last echo dies within our ears;
   A rose choked in the grass; an hour of fears;
   The gusts that past a darkening shore do beat;

The burst of music down an unlistening street—
I wonder at the idleness of tears.
Ye old, old dead, and ye of yesternight,
Chieftains, and bards, and keepers of the sheep,
By every cup of sorrow that you had,
Loose me from tears, and make me see aright
How each hath back what once he stayed to weep;
Homer his sight, David his little lad!
                    —Lizette Woodworth Reese.

SOMETIMES

Across the fields of yesterday
    He sometimes comes to me,
A little lad just back from play—
    The lad I used to be.

And yet he smiles so wistfully
    Once he has crept within,
I wonder if he hopes to see
    The man I might have been.
                    —Thomas S. Jones, Jr.

OFT IN THE STILLY NIGHT

Oft in the stilly night,
    Ere slumber's chain has bound me,
Fond Memory brings the light
    Of other days around me:
        The smiles, the tears,
        Of boyhood years,
    The words of love then spoken;
        The eyes that shone
        Now dimmed and gone,
    The cheerful hearts now broken.
Thus in the stilly night,
    Ere slumber's chain has bound me,
Sad Memory brings the light
    Of other days around me.

When I remember all
    The friends so linked together
I've seen around me fall,
    Like leaves in wintry weather,
        I feel like one
        Who treads alone
Some banquet-hall deserted,
    Whose lights are fled,
    Whose garlands dead,
And all but he departed.
Thus in the stilly night,
    Ere slumber's chain has bound me
Sad Memory brings the light
    Of other days around me.
                    —Thomas Moore.

THE OLD FAMILIAR FACES

I have had playmates, I have had companions,
In my days of childhood, in my joyful school-days,
All, all are gone, the old familiar faces.

I have been laughing, I have been carousing,
Drinking late, sitting late, with my bosom cronies,
All, all are gone, the old familiar faces.

I loved a love once, fairest among women;
Closed are her doors on me, I must not see her—
All, all are gone, the old familiar faces.

I have a friend, a kinder friend has no man;
Like an ingrate, I left my friend abruptly;
Left him, to muse on the old familiar faces.

Ghost-like I paced round the haunts of my childhood.
Earth seemed a desert I was bound to traverse,
Seeking to find the old familiar faces.

Friend of my bosom, thou more than a brother,
Why wert not thou born in my father's dwelling?
So might we talk of the old familiar faces—

How some they have died, and some they have left me
And some are taken from me; all are departed;
All, all are gone, the old familiar faces.

—Charles Lamb.

RABBI BEN EZRA

Grow old along with me!
The best is yet to be,
The last of life, for which the first was made:
Our times are in his hand
Who saith, "A whole I planned,
Youth shows but half; trust God: see all, nor be afraid!"

—Robert Browning.

BIRTHDAYS

It's only as a memory
  That you grow old.
Your body is an annual
  Like Marigold.
Your friends remember you the best
  By deeds, not years,
By joys you scatter on the way
  To banish tears.
It's not the years that count as much
  As how you live.
It's not the things you got from life
  But what you give.

—Anita Jackson.

AGE

Age is a quality of mind.
If you have left your dreams behind,
    If love is cold,
If you no longer look ahead,
If your ambition's fires are dead—
    Then you are old.

But if from life you take the best,
And if in life you keep the jest,
    If love you hold,
No matter how the years go by,
No matter how the birthdays fly—
    You are not old.

                                —Unknown.

MISER

I have seen many things,
    Too beautiful for words;
Twilight tremulous with mist—
    Birds.

I have heard music
    That was to me
Soft as the clinging fingers
    Of the sea.

I have known many things,
    Now I am old—
I am a miser
    Counting my gold.

                                —Harold Vinal.

THE OLD MAN AND JIM

Old man never had much to say—
   'Ceptin' to Jim,—
And Jim was the wildest boy he had—
   And the Old man jes' wrapped up in him!
Never heerd him speak but once
Er twice in my life,—and first time was
When the army broke out, and Jim he went,
The Old man backin' him, fer three months.—
And all 'at I heerd the Old man say
Was, jes' as we turned to start away,—
   "Well, good-bye, Jim:
   Take keer of vourse'f!"

'Peard-like, he was more satisfied
   Jes' *lookin'* at Jim,
And likin' him all to hisse'f-like, see?—
   'Cause he was jes' wrapped up in him!
And over and over I mind the day
The Old man come and stood round in the way
While we was drillin', a-watchin' Jim—
And down at the deepot a-heerin' him say,—
   "Well, good-bye, Jim:
   Take keer of yourse'f!"

Never was nothin' about the farm
   Disting'ished Jim;—
Neighbors all ust to wonder why
   The Old man 'peared wrapped up in him:
But when Cap. Biggler, he writ back,
'At Jim was the bravest boy we had
In the whole dern rigiment, white er black,
And his fightin' good as his farmin' bad—
'At he had led, with a bullet clean
Bored through his thigh, and carried the flag

Through the bloodiest battle you ever seen,—
The Old man wound up a letter to him
'At Cap. read to us, 'at said,—"Tell Jim
   Good-bye;
    And take keer of hisse'f!"

Jim come back jes' long enough
   To take the whim
'At he'd like to go back in the cavelry—
   And the Old man jes' wrapped up in him!—
Jim 'lowed 'at he'd had sich luck afore,
Guessed he'd tackle her three years more.
And the Old man gave him a colt he'd raised
And follered him over to Camp Ben Wade,
And laid around for a week er so,
Watchin' Jim on dress-parade—
Tel finally he rid away,
And last he heerd was the Old man say,—
   "Well, good-bye, Jim:
    Take keer of yourse'f!"

Tuk the papers, the Old man did,
   A-watchin' for Jim—
Fully believin' he'd make his mark
   Some way—jes' wrapped up in him!—
And many a time the word 'u'd come
'At stirred him up like the tap of a drum—
At Petersburg, fer instance, where
Jim rid right into their cannons there,
And tuk 'em, and p'inted 'em t'other way,
And socked it home to the boys in grey,
As they skotted fer timber, and on and on—
Jim a lieutenant and one arm gone,
And the Old man's words in his mind all day,—
   "Well, good-bye, Jim:
    Take keer of yourse'f!"

Think of a private, now, perhaps,
   We'll say like Jim,
'At's clumb clean up to the shoulder-straps—
   And the Old man jes' wrapped up in him!
Think of him—with the war plum' through,
And the glorious old Red-White-and-Blue
A-laughin' the news down over Jim,
And the Old man, bendin' over him—
The surgeon turnin' away with tears
'At hadn't leaked fer years and years—
As the hand of the dyin' boy clung to
His father's, the old voice in his ears,—
   "Well, good-bye, Jim:
   Take keer of yourse'f!"

                    —James Whitcomb Riley.

PRAYER FOR LAUGHTER

Dear Lord, to preserve my sanity
Midst chaos which threatens to swallow me
Help me, no matter what ill fate brings,
To look for the funny side of things!
Help me, above all else, to keep
My sense of humor when I would weep.
Let not my fellow-men cause distress;
Lord, make me to realize their funniness!
Help me to find the humor in pain
That throbs all day in my tired brain—
(To keep me constantly well aware
Of the brain's oft-doubted presence there!)
Send me a hearty laugh to calm
My quivering nerves with its magic balm . . .
And when Death comes, with lugubrious mien,
O Lord, may I chuckle with mirth serene
That a dour old spook as dread as he
Should be the means of releasing me!

                    —Madeline Slade.

PROOF

If radio's slim fingers
    Can pluck a melody
From night, and toss it over
    A continent or sea;

If the petaled white notes
    Of a violin
Are blown across a mountain,
    Or a city's din;

If songs, like crimson roses,
    Are plucked from thin blue air,
Why should mortals wonder
    If God hears prayer?
                    —Ethel Romig Fuller.

DEATH

Death stands above me, whispering low
    I know not what into my ear;
Of his strange language all I know
    Is, there is not a word of fear.
                    —Walter Savage Landor.

PROSPICE

Fear death?—to feel the fog in my throat,
    The mist in my face,
When the snows begin, and the blasts denote
    I am nearing the place,
The power of the night, the press of the storm,
    The post of the foe;
Where he stands, the Arch Fear in a visible form,
    Yet the strong man must go:

For the journey is done and the summit attained,
   And the barriers fall,
Though a battle's to fight ere the guerdon be gained,
   The reward of it all.
I was ever a fighter, so—one fight more,
   The best and the last!
I would hate that death bandaged my eyes, and forbore
   And bade me creep past.
No! let me taste the whole of it, fare like my peers
   The heroes of old,
Bear the brunt, in a minute pay glad life's arrears
   Of pain, darkness and cold.
For sudden the worst turns the best to the brave,
   The black minute's at end,
And the elements' rage, the fiend-voices that rave,
   Shall dwindle, shall blend,
Shall change, shall become first a peace out of pain,
   Then a light, then thy breast,
O thou soul of my soul! I shall clasp thee again,
   And with God be the rest!

—Robert Browning.

THE GRASS

A child said, *What is the grass?* fetching it to me with
   full hands;
How could I answer the child? I do not know what it is
   any more than he.

I guess it must be the flag of my disposition, out of
   hopeful green stuff woven.

Or I guess it is the handkerchief of the Lord,
A scented gift and remembrancer designedly dropt,
Bearing the owner's name someway in the corners, that
   we may see and remark, and say *Whose?*

Or I guess the grass is itself a child, the produced babe of
the vegetation.

Or I guess it is a uniform hieroglyphic,
And it means, sprouting alike in broad zones and narrow
zones,
Growing among black folks as among white,
Kanuck, Tuckahoe, Congressman, Cuff, I give them the
same, I receive them the same.

And now it seems to me the beautiful uncut hair of
graves.
Tenderly will I use your curling grass,
It may be you transpire from the breasts of young men,
It may be if I had known them I would have loved them,
It may be you are from old people, or from offspring
taken soon out of their mothers' laps,
And here you are the mothers' laps.

This grass is very dark to be from the white heads of
old mothers,
Darker than the colourless beards of old men,
Dark to come from under the faint red roofs of mouths.
O I perceive after all so many uttering tongues,
And I perceive they do not come from the roofs of mouths
for nothing.

I wish I could translate the hints about the dead young
men and women,
And the hints about old men and mothers, and the
offspring taken soon out of their laps.

What do you think has become of the young and old
men?
And what do you think has become of the women and
children?

They are alive and well somewhere,
The smallest sprout shows there is really no death,
And if ever there was it led forward life, and does not
  wait at the end to arrest it,
And ceas'd the moment life appear'd.

All goes onward and outward, nothing collapses,
And to die is different from what anyone supposed, and
  luckier.

—Walt Whitman.

UP-HILL

Does the road wind up-hill all the way?
  Yes, to the very end.
Will the day's journey take the whole long day?
  From morn to night, my friend.

But is there for the night a resting-place?
  A roof for when the slow dark hours begin,
May not the darkness hide it from my face?
  You cannot miss that inn.

Shall I meet other wayfarers at night?
  Those who have gone before.
Then must I knock, or call when just in sight?
  They will not keep you standing at that door.

Shall I find comfort, travel-sore and weak?
  Of labour you shall find the sum.
Will there be beds for me and all who seek?
  Yes, beds for all who come.

—Christina Georgina Rossetti.

→»«←

My love to all that I love:
  My love to all those that love me;
My love to all those that love those that I love;
  And to all those that love those that love me.

—Unknown.

GOOD-BYE

Good-bye, proud world! I'm going home:
Thou art not my friend, and I'm not thine.
Long through thy weary crowds I roam;
A river-ark on the ocean brine,
Long I've been tossed like the driven foam;
But now, proud world! I'm going home.

Good-bye to Flattery's fawning face;
To Grandeur with his wise grimace;
To upstart Wealth's averted eye;
To supple Office, low and high;
To crowded halls, to court and street;
To frozen hearts and hasting feet;
To those who go, and those who come;
Good-bye, proud world! I'm going home.

I am going to my own hearth-stone,
Bosomed in yon green hills alone,—
A secret nook in a pleasant land,
Whose groves the frolic fairies planned;
Where arches green, the livelong day,
Echo the blackbird's roundelay,
And vulgar feet have never trod
A spot that is sacred to thought and God.

O, when I am safe in my sylvan home,
I tread on the pride of Greece and Rome;
And when I am stretched beneath the pines,
Where the evening star so holy shines,
I laugh at the lore and the pride of man,
At the sophist schools and the learned clan·
For what are they all, in their high conceit,
When man in the bush with God may meet?
                    —Ralph Waldo Emerson.

THE SOLDIER

If I should die, think only this of me:
  That there's some corner of a foreign field
That is forever England. There shall be
  In that rich earth a richer dust concealed;
A dust, whom England bore, shaped, made aware,
  Gave, once, her flowers to love, her ways to roam,
A body of England's, breathing English air,
  Washed by the rivers, blest by suns of home.
And think, this heart, all evil shed away,
  A pulse in the eternal mind, no less
    Gives somewhere back the thoughts by England
      given;
Her sights and sounds; dreams happy as her day;
  And laughter, learnt of friends; and gentleness,
    In hearts at peace, under an English heaven.
                                        —Rupert Brooke.

SO BE MY PASSING

  A late lark twitters from the quiet skies
  And from the west,
  Where the sun, his day's work ended,
  Lingers as in content,
  There falls on the old, gray city
  An influence luminous and serene,
  A shining peace.

  The smoke ascends
  In a rosy-and-golden haze. The spires
  Shine and are changed. In the valley
  Shadows rise. The lark sings on. The sun,
  Closing his benediction,

Sinks, and the darkening air
Thrills with a sense of the triumphing night—
Night with her train of stars
And her great gift of sleep.

So be my passing!
My task accomplish'd, and the long day done,
My wages taken, and in my heart
Some late lark singing,
Let me be gather'd to the quiet west,
The sundown splendid and serene,
Death.

—William Ernest Henley.

POISE

You will end life just as you close a favorite book,
    Turn off the shaded light and slowly climb the stairs.
With you there'll be no startled cry, no wondering look
    When you behold the Room you've entered unawares.

—Violet Alleyn Storey.

HERE LIES

Here lies an old woman who always was tired.
She lived in a house where help was not hired.
Her last words on earth were: "Dear friends, I am going
Where washing ain't done, nor sweeping, nor sewing.
But everything there is exact to my wishes,
For where they don't eat there's no washing of dishes.
I'll be where glad anthems forever are ringing,
But having no voice, I'll be clear of the singing.
Don't mourn for me now, don't mourn for me never,
I'm going to do nothing for ever and ever."

—An epitaph in Pembroke, Massachusetts.

LIFE

.   .   .   .

Life! we've been long together,
Through pleasant and through cloudy weather;
  'Tis hard to part when friends are dear;
  Perhaps 'twill cost a sigh, a tear;
  Then steal away, give little warning,
    Choose thine own time,
Say not "Good-night," but in some brighter clime
    Bid me "Good-morning."

              —Anna Letitia Barbauld.

12. TAPS

Taps

>»>«<

HAVING run out of bugle calls and almost out of pages, I too may just as well run out on you and call it a day.

If some of the chapter titles have seemed a little strained, think nothing of it. It was an old bugle. If some of the bugle calls have been out of order, pay no attention. It was a new bugler.

Seriously though, I hope you noticed that there was no bugle call included which might be used to sound "Defeat." You can't blow that on our trumpet. It's old, but not that old.

Anyway this is a book of magic, all the magic there is in poetry, and to prove it, here is the "Hocus Pocus," the "Sim-Sali-Bim," the "Presto Chango" we said over this book when we started it out on its way, knowing some day it would reach you. . . .

ENVOY

Go, little book, and wish to all
Flowers in the garden, meat in the hall,
A bin of wine, a spice of wit,
A house with lawns enclosing it,
A living river by the door,
A nightingale in the sycamore!
—Robert Louis Stevenson.

This was the magic verse we said over the book because we knew that with all of these things you would find it would be no trick at all to . . . "Pack up Your Troubles."

Acknowledgments

The editor and publishers of *Pack Up Your Troubles* wish to express their appreciation to the following publishers, agents, and authors for permission to reprint their poems:

The Atlanta Constitution and Mrs. Frank L. Stanton for "A Hopeful Brother," "A Poor Unfortunate," "Constancy," "This World," "A Pretty Good World," and "Jest A-Wearyin' Fer You" by Frank L. Stanton.

The Bobbs-Merrill Company for "The Old Man and Jim" by James Whitcomb Riley.

Berton Braley for "Success."

Gelett Burgess for "Willy and the Lady."

Mrs. William Herbert Carruth for "Each in His Own Tongue" by William Herbert Carruth.

W. B. Conkey Company for "Worth While" by Ella Wheeler Wilcox.

Covici, Friede, Inc., for selections from "The Cheerful Cherub" by Rebecca McCann.

Dodge Publishing Company for "Father" by Edmund Vance Cooke.

Dodd Mead & Company, Inc., for "Soldier" by Rupert Brooke; "The Cremation of Sam McGee" and "The Quitter" by Robert W. Service; and excerpts from "Vagabond's House" by Don Blanding.

Doubleday, Doran & Company, Inc., for "Bill of Fare" and "The Raspberry Tree" by Stoddard King; "Noah, Jonah an' Cap'n John Smith" by Don Marquis;

and "Gunga Din" and "If" by Rudyard Kipling, with special permission from A. P. Watt Co., Ltd., London.

John L. Foley for "Sometimes" and "Youth," by Thomas S. Jones, Jr.

Mrs. Zulime Taft Garland for "Do You Fear the Wind?" by Hamlin Garland.

Greenberg, Publisher, Inc., for "Sir Murgatroyd of Sebastapool" by Joseph Newman.

The Goldsmith-Woolard Publishing Company for "An Explanation" by Walter Learned.

Harcourt, Brace and Company for "The People, Yes" by Carl Sandburg.

Houghton Mifflin for "Lost City" by Marion Strobel.

J. B. Lippincott Company for "My Pipe" by Christopher Morley.

Liveright Publishing Corporation for selections from "Poems in Praise of Practically Nothing" by Samuel Hoffenstein.

Lothrop, Lee & Shepard Company for "The Prayer of Cyrus Brown" and "The House by the Side of the Road" by Samuel Walter Foss.

The Macmillan Company for "Mr. Flood's Party" by Edwin Arlington Robinson.

Mrs. Douglas Malloch for "You Have to Believe" by Douglas Malloch.

Virgil Markham for "Outwitted" and "Preparedness" by Edwin Markham.

L. C. Page & Company for "Building the Bridge for Him" by W. A. Dromgoole.

The Pilgrim Press for "The Ways" by John Oxenham.

George Palmer Putnam for "Courage" by Amelia Earhart.

Roberts Brothers for "Fate" by Susan M. Spalding.

Charles Scribner's Sons for "I Have a Rendezvous with Death" by Alan Seegar; "The Lacquer Liquor

Locker" by David McCord; and "Work" by Henry van Dyke.

The Viking Press for "Parable for a Certain Virgin" by Dorothy Parker; and "The Insulting Letter" by William Ellery Leonard.

Yale University Press for "Miser" by Harold Vinal.

Unless otherwise noted, permissions for the use of poems in this book were granted by the authors themselves.

Index

⟫⟩⟨⟨

    * Quoted in part.

* Quoted in part.

* Quoted in part.

*Quoted in part.

* Quoted in part.

    *Quoted in part.

*Quoted in part.

* Quoted in part.

* Quoted in part.